OFF PATROL

MEMORIES OF B.C. PROVINCIAL POLICEMEN

Kamloops Detachment in the early 1940s. Seated at center is Inspector Barber who as a Sergeant in 1926 opened a Police Post in the wilderness around Fort Nelson. (See page 48.)

FRONT COVER

On horseback and snowshoes, by dog team and motor launch, cars and aircraft, B.C.'s Provincial policemen maintained law and order.
The vessel is *PML (Police Motor Launch) 14*, largest of the police boats. Used on Vancouver Island's West Coast, the well named "Graveyard of the Pacific," she was equipped with a courtroom and cells.

BACK COVER

Constable Bob Pyper at Soda Creek lockup in the early 1900s. Although abandoned, the lockup still stands. (See page 65.)
Chartres Brew, the Force's first commander, is buried in Barkerville's historic cemetery. The epitaph is believed to have been written by Judge Matthew Baillie Begbie. (See page 11.)

PHOTO CREDITS
B.C. Provincial Archives, 6, 7, 12, 16, 21, 26, 35, 68, 69, 81, 97, 104/5, 109, 112/113, 115, 119, 122, 131, 141, 144; *The Shoulder Strap*, 4, 13, 10, 16, 21, 28, 45, 49, 55, 68, 69, 73, 94, 109, 122, 128, 129, 131, 150; Tourism B.C., 7; Vancouver City Archives, 94, 130; Vancouver Public Library, 34, 136, 140; Cecil Clark, 40; R.W. Purdy, 78, 81, 84, 85, 88, 90, 118, 119.

Copyright © 1991 B.C. Provincial Police Veterans' Association

Canadian Cataloguing in Publication Data

Main entry under title:
Off patrol

ISBN 0-919214-85-1

1. British Columbia Provincial Police—Biography.
2. Police—British Columbia—Biography.
HV8159.B7033 1991   363.2'092'2   C91-091032-4

Heritage House Publishing Company Ltd.
Box 1228, Station A, Surrey, B.C. V3S 2B3

Printed in Canada

CONTENTS

ACKNOWLEDGMENTS

Most of the material in this book is from *Off Patrol*, a quarterly newsletter published by the B.C. Provincial Police Veterans' Association from 1980 to 1984. (Off Patrol was an informal expression used by police officers when they were off duty and at leisure to swap experiences.) The 17 issues of the newsletter contain an invaluable record of police experiences from the days when Mainland B.C. was a roadless wilderness to the jet age.

Credit for the success of *Off Patrol* goes to its editor, Senior Clerk-Corporal P. H. "Spike" Brown. He spent 16 years on the Force and after his retirement devoted hundreds of hours to the publication. He was a talented cartoonist and artist, many of his cartoons appearing in *The Shoulder Strap*, official publication of the Provincial Police. Spike died in 1983 and the newsletter soon afterward.

The Shoulder Strap to which Spike contributed his cartoons contains probably the best collection of photos and articles on the B.C. Provincial Police. At one time, however, the most extensive collection was at the Force's Victoria Headquarters where thousands of photos, letters and other first-person material were an irreplaceable source of information. But for some unfathomable reason when the RCMP took over virtually all records were destroyed. Because of this destruction, many photos in this book had to be copied from *The Shoulder Strap*, resulting in loss of quality.

The magazine was founded in 1938 by Albert "Brookie" Brookhouse as a hobby, with one-half of the profits going to the Police Rewards Fund. From the first issue Brookie established a standard that matched the best tradition of the Force. He devoted all of his spare time to *The Shoulder Strap*, not only maintaining the quality but improving it through the nine years he published before his death in 1948. Afterward new owners took over the magazine but it died after a few issues.

Associated with the magazine from its first issue as an editor was Inspector Cecil Clark who joined the Force in 1916. He served 35 years, retiring as Assistant Commissioner when the RCMP took over. During his long service — over one-third of the Force's life — and after he retired in 1950, Cecil became the Force's unofficial historian.

He was a familiar figure in the Provincial Archives, searching through thousands of copies of the province's newspapers and other documents. He wrote scores of articles about cases in which the police were involved. Most of them were published in the *Victoria Colonist* and were popular year after year. From his series came three books: *Tales of the B.C. Provincial Police*, now out of print, and *Stories of the B.C. Provincial Police — Volumes One and Two*. Both are still in print and have reached best-seller status. Several of Cecil's articles are in this book.

Another valuable publication is *92 Years of Pride*, also out of print. It is a booklet published in 1983 by the Okanagan Division of the RCMP Veterans' Association as a tribute to the B.C. Provincial Police. Essentially a concise, well-illustrated history, it was compiled by *Off Patrol* editor Spike Brown and is a valuable contribution to the Force's history.

Top left: Deputy Commissioner Cecil Clark, a 35-year veteran of the B.C. Provincial Police and the Force's unofficial historian.

Above: Albert Brookhouse, founder of *The Shoulder Strap*, the Force's official magazine.

Left: Corporal P. H. "Spike" Brown, editor of the Police Veterans' newsletter, *Off Patrol*.

For permission to reprint material from *Off Patrol* the publisher thanks the B.C. Provincial Police Veterans' Association. Special thanks go to members Jack Meek for his aid and to J. W. Purdy for letting us copy photos from his Cassiar album to illustrate his and Jack Meek's articles in this book.

We also thank the *Victoria Colonist* (now the *Times-Colonist*) for permission to reprint Cecil Clark's articles on pages 20 and 28, and the staff of the Provincial Archives in Victoria. As always, they were friendly and helpful, as were staff of the Vancouver Public Library.

NINETY-TWO YEARS OF PRIDE

From its founding on November 19, 1858, to its transfer to the RCMP on August 15, 1950, the B.C. Provincial Police earned a North America-wide recognition for dedication and efficiency. Its record is still remembered with pride by those who served.

by Assistant Commissioner Cecil Clark

I joined the B.C. Provincial Police in 1916, then was to spend 35 years in the Force. What was it like? Well, on my first day at Headquarters in Victoria a horse and buggy arrived, driven by Constable Macdonald of the Sidney Detachment. He had come 20 miles to deliver his monthly returns. In those days the police owned no transportation, although next year we were the proud possessor of two Model T Fords, one in Victoria and one in Vancouver. We had one telephone in the central office, with a sort of party line from it to the Superintendent's office.

The office routine at Victoria? Well, the letters, scores of them, were done on a typewriter. In the evening they were put into letter books which were volumes with thin rice paper in which were interleaved

The first officer to die on duty was John Ogilvie, above, murdered at Bella Coola in 1865.

In 1858 Crimean war veteran Chartres Brew, top right, became the Force's first commanding officer.

Roger Peachey, opposite, a World War One veteran who lost a leg and won the Military Cross, was the commanding officer when the B.C. Provincial Police became part of the RCMP in 1950

The Force's heritage dates back to November 19, 1858, when the Crown Colony of British Columbia was born at Fort Langley. The ceremony took place in the Fort's "Big House," opposite page, now restored and open to visitors.

the letters with damp cloths. They were then put in a press, such being a contraption with a big lever which was screwed down. By this means the letters were imprinted on the thin rice paper. Pressure was exerted for five minutes, then the press was unscrewed. The letters, now being damp, were spread around to dry.

Since there was no filing system, the incoming letters were, in their volumes or binders, placed in a cabinet. If you wanted to see them and the answers you looked up an index. So, we went to and fro, from question to answer, from filing cabinet to letter book. It was a cumbersome arrangement. But we didn't know any better because there was nothing better. And such were the distances and transportation facilities that it could take four months or more for a policeman to get a reply to a letter.

Part of my duty was to help take sick or injured sailors from the naval base at Esquimalt to hospital. When I received a call, I would walk four blocks to Victoria Transfer where a horse-drawn "ambulance" was waiting with a driver. Then we'd be off to Esquimalt with a gong going "clang, clang," sounded by the driver with his foot.

Neither the driver nor I had any knowledge of first aid except the rudimentary outline I had learned in the Boy Scouts. There was no stretcher in this covered wagon, but anyway we'd get the injured man to hospital, a journey of several rough miles.

Next morning maybe Inspector Frank Murray would come out of his office and accost me with, "Clark, that man you brought in from Esquimalt isn't going to live. Go get his dying statement."

So, I went to do as I was ordered. It seemed I was continuously getting dying statements, mainly because I had the facility of shorthand. At the age of 17 I began to imagine I was a deathbed counsellor!

Salaries? Constables got $65 a month, old-timers in the force soared to $75. But you could get a T-bone steak with French fries and other vegetables, coffee and pie, for 50 cents. Problem was we couldn't charge a meal over 35 cents.

When I joined the B.C. Provincial force it was then nearing the half century in age. It had the distinction of being not only the first police force in what is now Western Canada, but also Canada's oldest territorial force. When it was formed in 1858 there wasn't a mile of road on what is today the B.C. mainland, the Prairie was a lawless region known as Rupert's Land, while Canada was the name given to a small corridor along the St. Lawrence River to the Great Lakes. When the provinces of Alberta and Saskatchewan were created in 1905, the B.C. Police force was already nearly 50 years old, and in 1912 when Ontario and Quebec attained their present boundaries it had been upholding the law for 54 years.

During the almost century-long era that the B.C. Provincial Police were the front line of law and order they were always few in number. Even by 1900 there were only 100 to police an area larger than Washington, Oregon and California combined. They nevertheless maintained the peace and well, with 13 sacrificing their lives in the line of duty. The first was Constable J. B. Ogilvie at Bella Coola in May 1865, the last was Constable Frank Clark at Victoria in November 1941.

For decades horses were the main means of travel in summer, with weeks in the saddle not uncommon. In winter snowshoes and dog teams were used throughout the northern one-half of B.C. since there were virtually no roads. It wasn't unusual for a lone Constable on dog-team patrol to cover 400 and more miles and be out several weeks in the sub-zero cold and blizzards of northern B.C.

Other policemen were adept with tiller and mainsail as they patrolled B.C.'s 7,000-mile coastline. Then in the 1890s came launches with open naphtha engines which were gradually replaced by a fleet of diesel-powered cruisers. Finally arrived the air age and some officers piloted planes.

The Force's heritage dates to 1858 when gold was discovered on the Fraser River. That spring an avalanche of some 30,000 miners over the next few months changed the land forever. Until then what is today Mainland B.C. was controlled by the Hudson's Bay Company and generally known as New Caledonia. The only sign of white inhabitants were the Bay's fur trading posts linked by trails and supplied by brigades of pack horses. They included Fort Langley, Fort Kamloops, Fort George and Fort St. James.

Headquarters was on southern Vancouver Island at Fort Victoria, (today B.C.'s capital of Victoria). At the time Vancouver Island was a Crown Colony controlled by England, with James Douglas as Governor and a white population of about 800, some 300 at Fort Victoria. Into this quiet backwater of Empire stampeded the hopeful miners, most of them from California where the law was largely upheld by the six-gun and citizens' vigilante groups. For this reason the newcomers were virtually all armed. As one writer noted, each had "...the universal revolver, many of them carrying a brace of such, as well as a bowie knife."

Since there were no police to keep order, Governor James Douglas and British authorities were fearful that the incoming miners would clamor to have the region made part of the U.S. On July 7, 1858, Governor Douglas met the situation by appointing Augustus F. Pemberton as Commissioner of Police for Vancouver Island. Under Pemberton were a Superintendent, Chief Constable, Sergeant and five Constables. To control such a vast influx their numbers were pitifully few but they succeeded. That summer in Victoria the belt gun was banned which meant that the newcomers couldn't walk around carrying their beloved six-guns.

On the Mainland for several months of that hectic spring, summer and fall there wasn't even one lawman. To organize a constabulary, Britain's Colonial Secretary despatched 43-year-old Sub-Inspector Chartres Brew of the Royal Irish Constabulary. Immediately on Brew's arrival, Governor Douglas appointed him Chief Inspector of Police. The date was November 19, 1858, the swearing-in ceremony at Fort Langley on the Fraser River just east of today's Vancouver. At the same ceremony the Colony of British Columbia was born, with James

1

2

3

Many policemen were veterans, beginning with the
Crimean War. In World War Two about one-third of
B.C. Provincials enlisted, although they were classed
as an essential service and discouraged from leaving.

4

1   Jack Meek — see pages 78 and 118 — joined the RCAF
and won the Conspicuous Gallantry Medal and the
Distinguished Flying Cross. He still carries a bullet
near his heart from a German fighter plane.

2   Harold Calvert joined the RCAF and was shot down
over Germany in 1942. While trying to escape, he was
killed by the Nazis.

3   A. L. Frost won the Military Medal while serving with
the Canadian Scottish Regiment.

4   Alan Drysdale, killed while serving with Ferry
Command, was one of over 17,000 Canadian airmen
who died during World War Two.

5   As a bomber pilot, J. R. McDonald completed 62
missions and won the Distinguished Service Order
and the Distinguished Flying Cross.

5

Douglas becoming governor of both British Columbia and Vancouver Island.

Brew's first duty was to survey conditions first-hand in the vicinity of the gold strike and report to the Governor. His findings prompted him to suggest the need for 150 members of the Irish Constabulary, to be brought immediately to the Colony. The Secretary of State vetoed the suggestion, feeling that the revenues of the Colony would not permit the transportation and maintenance of such a body. He recommended instead that local people be recruited.

At the end of 1859 the Colony was divided into six administrative districts. Overseeing each was a Magistrate who could hire six policeman of his choice and who had total power, including punishing offenders. A problem with the system was that there was no central control of the police — or the Magistrates. The solution was to appoint Chartres Brew Gold Commissioner, effectively putting him in overall charge. In 1864 there was another move toward centralization when all appointments to the constabulary had to have the Governor's approval.

By then Brew's handful of locally recruited policemen had extended their activities to a new gold strike on Williams Creek in the Cariboo Country. Later they were on hand when a fresh bonanza was uncovered at Wild Horse Creek in the southeast corner of the Colony. Thereafter, whenever a miner found gold, a policeman was soon at his elbow.

Despite the fact that miners outnumbered policemen by hundreds — and even thousands — to one, there was remarkably little lawlessness. Hubert Howe Bancroft, the Pacific Northwest's foremost historian, observed: "Never in the pacification and settlement of any section of America have there been so few disturbances, so few crimes against life and property."

After nearly 12 years of faithful service to the Colony, Chartres Brew died on May 31, 1870, at Richfield in the Cariboo. He was buried in the cemetery at Barkerville and is commemorated by Mt. Brew on the north side of beautiful Quesnel Lake in the Cariboo Mountains.

By then the Colonies of British Columbia and Vancouver Island had been united with police headquarters changed from New Westminster to Victoria. Then in 1871 there was another change. The Colonies became the Province of British Columbia, part of a new nation called Canada. Brew's Colonial police were now the B.C. Provincial Police. Two years later the North-West Mounted Police (today's RCMP) was formed and made the red serge the symbol of law and order on Canada's Central Plains. By then, however, their B.C. counterpart had been upholding justice west of the Rockies for 15 years.

As the province slowly grew — at Confederation its white population was only 9,000 — the Force expanded, but also slowly. In 1895, for instance, there were only 70 Constables scattered about the entire province, many doing very little police work. The bulk of their duties was collecting revenue, assessment of taxes and government agent's

In the pioneer era a policeman was usually responsible for a territory larger than some European countries. In northern B.C., one-man wilderness dog team patrols of 300 or more miles were considered routine. In summer horses replaced the dogs.

Above is Constable Gordon J. Duncan at Pouce Coupe in 1914, his beat the Peace River country. The police station behind him was built of lumber brought by horses 100 miles from the nearest sawmill in Alberta.

work in general. For instance, there was William Stephenson. He was stationed at Quesnelle Forks in the Cariboo. Besides being a Constable, he was also Mining Recorder, Collector of Revenue, and Justice of the Peace. He also acted as District Magistrate, and therefore could not do any actual police work.

Then there was Bill Parker at the 150 Mile House on the Cariboo Wagon Road. Bill patrolled the wagon road from Soda Creek to Bridge Creek during the summer months, nearly a 200-mile round trip. He was not paid during the winter, and had to provide his own horse and hotel expenses, as well as fodder and stabling for his horse. For all this he received during the summer $125 per month.

Another was Fred Wollaston, also stationed at the 150 Mile Post. He was a Special Constable on duty as a stagecoach guard. Millions of dollars in gold from the Barkerville area were sent by stage, and to discourage bandits, a police officer rode with the driver. He got $125 a month and had to furnish his own hotel accommodation and all personal expenses. Like Parker, he was only paid during the summer.

William G. McMynn, who later became Superintendent of the Force, was stationed at Midway where he was Mining Recorder, Collector of Revenue and Constable at $75 per month. As he had very little

Uniforms were introduced in 1924, greatly increasing pride among the men and respect of the public. Above is the B.C. Provincial Police Revolver No. 1 Team in 1945. They had just won the B.C. Pistol Championship for the fifth consecutive year.

Members are, from left, Sub-Inspector Cecil Clark, Constable Walter Bailey, Corporal J. A. Young, Constable Jack Henry, and Corporal W. Conlon.

time to devote to police work in view of his other appointments, Constable Ralph W. Deans was his assistant at a salary of $60 per month.

But not all Constables received such "high" wages. There was Fred Heal. He was a Special Constable at Victoria doing daily rural patrol work. He furnished his own horse and buggy and was paid $30 a month. In the Cariboo at Clinton Constable George Mitchell also received $30 a month.

To police the West Coast of Vancouver Island there were two Constables, Stanley Spain and James Seeley. These men were stationed at Clayoquot. To patrol their long and rugged coast line, they were furnished with a small sailing sloop which proved totally ineffective to cover the wild and rocky coast.

Accommodation for policemen ranged from basic to primitive. Many of them lived in the local lockup with their prisoners — everybody cosy in one room except that the prisoners had bars on their section. The one at Fort Steele in East Kootenay, for instance, like most was log, 33 feet long by 23 wide. It had the luxury of three rooms. The outer room was used by the police and also by the Public Works men who kept their tools in it. The inner room had three cells, and was also used as a kitchen. An adjoining room was used by Constable Barnes and his family. The logs were rotten and the wintry winds blew in through the chinks.

In addition, the Government was quite economical in those days. Bill Stephenson, Government Agent and Constable at Quesnelle Forks, thought a new lockup should be provided. Since a bridge was being taken down he had the sound timber brought up and used in the construction of the new quarters. The building cost the modest sum of $204.

But the one which Constable Jack Meek constructed at McDames Creek in the Cassiar in the 1930s was even more of a bargain. It cost a total of $20 for two windows — then Headquarters wouldn't pay for the windows because they "weren't necessary." (See page 118.)

As already noted, the policemen were always few in number — incredibly few. As Constable Anderson describes on page 97, many were responsible for a massive territory, often a roadless wilderness. For the first 40 or so years men in the field were very much on their own. They laid their own charges and prosecuted their own cases. There were even instances when they performed hangings.

On horseback in summer and snowshoes and dog teams in winter they travelled thousands of miles. Take only one policeman's experience. In 1897 Constable Robert Pyper was sent to Alexis Creek in the vast Chilcotin to open a Detachment. That Christmas he had a murder on his hands. A 17-year-old Chilcotin Indian called Samien shot and killed Lewis Elkin, a young Englishman who was running a trading store about 12 miles southwest of Tatla Lake. After the murder, Samien possessed himself of the storekeeper's keys, then fitted himself out with a new shirt, coat, pants and boots and took off for Nemish Valley on Elkin's horse. Somewhere along the trail he stole two fresh mounts to cover 60 miles in 14 hours.

But Samien couldn't resist boasting about his exploit. Word of the killing reached the dead man's brother, Ed, at Chilko Lake. He saddled up and got to the trading store on New Year's Eve. Here he found his brother's body slumped over the kitchen table, a bullet in the back of his head.

Elkin then rode 85 miles to Alexis Creek to tell Pyper who promptly left for the murder scene. His investigation completed, the policeman rode 120 miles until he caught up with his quarry. He held a preliminary hearing before Justice of the Peace Franklin, having already logged over 200 miles in the harsh Chilcotin January weather. Then he escorted his prisoner to 150 Mile House, temperature -20° F and a foot of snow on the ground. At 150 Mile House another Constable took Samien some 140 miles by stagecoach to Ashcroft where he boarded a train for the final 60-mile journey to Kamloops. On the way Samien failed in a break for liberty and ended up with a life sentence. As for Constable Pyper, when he finally reached Alexis Creek after the completion of his mission he had ridden some 400 wintry miles.

Even into the 1930s conditions in some areas hadn't changed much, especially the Chilcotin and northern B.C. That was when

Constable Stan Raybone and Game Warden Bill Broughten left Williams Lake for the Anahim Lake region on the track of two halfbreeds wanted for murder.

With a team and horses they left by sleigh on the first 200 miles. It took two weeks. Then they continued their search on snowshoes, knowing that the killers would shoot them on sight. They were unsuccessful, but in trying had travelled some 800 miles in winter conditions. In later years when Stan had retired as Inspector after 21 years in the Provincial force and 14 in the RCMP, I asked him how the trip was.

"Pretty tough," he said. In fact that was all he said.

In addition to chasing law breakers, a task which befell Constables was searching for missing people. Fiercely independent trappers and prospectors in particular had problems when old age crept up and they refused to change their life style. The article by Constable B. Jamieson on page 73 is an example.

Another instance of their independent attitude and the at times sad consequence was recorded at the Atlin Detachment in 1943. A watchman at the Tulsequah Mine reported that Jim MacGavin, an 82-year-old veteran prospector, had cremated himself in his log cabin.

The death was discovered when J. A. MacDonald, watchman at the Tulsequah Mine, found MacGavin's cabin burned to the ground. Mac-Gavin, still physically strong and active despite his 82 years, lived alone in the cabin 12 miles from Tulsequah in northwestern British Columbia near the Alaska border.

MacDonald found a letter dated January 1943 in a bottle hanging by a string in MacGavin's woodshed. The letter said:

"Very ill with appendix trouble. This is the finish. Have no way to get to doctor and too weak to get wood. Hate to do it but best way seems to call it off and cremate outfit. — Jim."

In addition to remarkably few men policing an area so huge that the distance, as the crow flies, from Atlin Detachment in northwest B.C. via Vancouver to Sparwood in southeast B.C. is equivalent to travelling from Vancouver through the U.S. into Mexico, there was another handicap. The officers were dressed in civilian clothes. When they enlisted they were provided with a baton, handcuffs, gun and badge. That was it. No training. They had to learn on the job. These conditions remained essentially unchanged until 1923 when the Police and Prisons Regulations Act came into force. Thereafter the force started on a program that was to make it one of the best — if not the best — law enforcement agencies in North America.

A khaki and green uniform was adopted, pay improved and the administrative structure changed. New ranks were Superintendent (later changed to Commissioner), Assistant Superintendent (also later changed to Assistant Commissioner,) Deputy Commissioner, Inspector, Sub-Inspector, Staff-Sergeant, Sergeant, Corporal, Detective, 1st, 2nd, and 3rd Class Constables, and Probationary Constable.

Out of the reorganization grew a system of policing municipalities under contract, a first for Canada. A Police Training School was started in Victoria in 1930 and a Criminal Investigation Branch established at

On patrol in the Peace River in 1937, the temperature -38°F.

Sergeant Carl Ledoux in 1928 with the first portable shortwave equipment used by any police force in North America.

Police Motor Launch 9 and the Force's first aircraft in 1949. The policemen began patrolling B.C.'s multi-thousand-mile coastline in 1895, their craft a 16-foot rowboat equipped with a sail.

Headquarters. Its specialists helped officers in the field to solve difficult crimes and it became part of a continent-wide clearing house for information on crimes and criminals.

Another first for North America was the use of radio which eventually gave all Detachments virtually instant contact with Headquarters. The police radio network was a homespun development. In 1928 Corporal Carl Ledoux demonstrated the practicability of short-wave radio on his home-made set. The demonstration was an immediate success and soon Ledoux had installations in Victoria, Vancouver, Nelson and Kamloops. Later the network was expanded to 22 stations, with other installations and operators on police boats.

The result was dramatic. At McDames Creek, for instance, the Constable in winter had to make a 500-mile round trip to Telegraph Creek by dog team for mail which could be a month or more old. Now communication was direct and instant.

The Force even developed portable radios. Carried like a small suitcase and weighing about 40 pounds, they could be used on dog-team patrols. The station took five minutes to assemble, each a complete sending and receiving unit which even included a pencil and message pad.

The radio was especially welcome to the Marine Division whose boats patrolled the province's 7,000 miles of coastline and were as isolated as any Northern outpost. The Division began very modestly with Constable A. D. Drummond patrolling the Gulf Islands in a rowboat. Then he was provided with a sail boat, the *Maybelle*. Since answering a call could take days if a contrary wind was blowing, the police heartily embraced the first motors, however cantankerous. Over the years the PML (Police Motor Launch) fleet grew until there were 14 boats from Vancouver to Prince Rupert.

Pride of the fleet was PML 14. She was 100 feet long and especially fitted to patrol Vancouver Island's West Coast, a treacherous area which caused hundreds of shipwrecks. Since her ports of call included many isolated coastal communities, her facilities included a courtroom and five cells. Her first skipper was Sergeant Harold Raybone who had been involved when two police officers were murdered in Prince Rupert. (See page 68.)

Another Division which found radios invaluable was the Highway Patrol, formed in 1935. Pavement was still in the future, the route of the "Highways" little changed from the original wagon and stagecoach roads of the province's frontier era. In 1929, for instance, Constable Bill Anderson was transferred to Nelson as one of the first motorcycle policemen. He picked up a new bike and sidecar in Vancouver and headed out. One dusty week later he reached Nelson.

But as population grew and roads were improved, the Highway Patrol expanded until vehicles were travelling several million miles a year. To increase efficiency the Highway Patrol equipment was standardized, one of the first police forces in North America to do so.

Records kept by the B.C. Police Motor Vehicle Branch show that in 1937, there were 114,528 vehicles registered in B.C., only 21 per cent of them in the Interior. There were 126 different makes of passenger vehicles and 132 of commercial. Can anyone name them? Best selling car was Ford, then Chevrolet, Plymouth and Dodge.

That year individual members of the Force travelled 2.6 million miles to uphold the law. Cars and motorbikes accounted for 1,757,000, horseback another 19,100, and foot slogging 250,000, the latter distance equal to ten times around the world.

Although horses, which for generations had been the main means of travel, were being used less and less, they still performed valuable service, with a Mounted Section formed in 1931. Stationed first in Victoria, it was later moved to Oakalla Prison Farm near Vancouver. The troop of horses provided escorts for distinguished guests and patrols for the more sparsely populated areas of the Lower Mainland. Many new recruits spent their first year or two with the Section, preparing themselves for Detachments in the Interior where horses were still a vital part of police work.

One government department which stemmed from the Provincial Police and with which the Force was closely affiliated for many years was the Game Branch. As noted in the booklet, *92 Years of Pride:*

"As early as 1859 there was legislation on Vancouver Island prohibiting the selling of game out of season and the shooting of it within the limits of a town, then meaning in essence, Victoria and Nanaimo. The police enforced the Game laws, although they were minimal in content and effect. Even as late as the 1890s Constable B. W. Anderson at Comox suggested there should be provisions to prevent dynamiting fish in lakes. He reported seeing one man driving a wagon load of fish so taken, and pointed out he had no power to stop such practices. Anderson also suggested that the selling of deer meat from door to door should be licensed.

"The game laws were indeed lax, for not long after the turn of the century a non-resident hunter was permitted for the fee of $50 to bag 10 deer, 3 caribou, 3 mountain sheep, 5 mountain goats, 2 moose and 2 elk! Also it was lawful to sell game in public markets. 'Shooting for the Market' caused ducks to be sold for 25 cents a pair, and there were cases such as 1,100 deer hides being sold to San Francisco, and a farmer at Princeton feeding his pigs on deer meat throughout the winter. Small wonder that there was growing demand to end such abuses, among them the serving of game in hotels and restaurants, on steamships and railway dining cars.

"In 1904 a special body was formed known as the Provincial Game Department, under much respected conservationist A. Bryan Williams. But a change in government in 1916 caused it to be replaced with the Game Conservation Board which was highly political and short-lived. Enforcement of game laws was again vested under the provincial police as the Game Branch, with Inspector Frank Butler in charge. In 1929 the Game Branch became a separate entity, a department of the provincial government, like the police directly responsible to the Attorney-General and later titled the Fish and Wildlife Service."

The last branch formed was the Air Division. On October 27, 1949, the Force received its first aircraft, a Beaver. The float plane, like the radio before it, greatly increased police effectiveness. Piloted by Sergeant Noel Beaumont, it was used for everything from mercy flights to regular police work. Its service, however, was brief. No, it didn't crash.

In 1950 the Provincial Government for "reasons of economy" turned policing duties over to the RCMP under contract. Of the Force's 511 members, 482 became Mounties. The B.C. Provincial Police became history.

During their almost century-long service the far ranging officers readily embraced anything new that would make them more efficient. The first instance was in 1866. A gambler named John Barry was wanted for the murder of Charles Blessing between Quesnel and Barkerville. Constable John H. Sullivan of the nearby Richfield Detachment set out on horseback after him. He rode 200 miles to Soda Creek south of Quesnel but Barry had caught a stagecoach and was on his way to Yale. Fortunately, the Collins around-the-world telegraph line was under construction. The single wire had just reached Soda Creek but was not in commercial use since it was still being tested.

Constable Sullivan persuaded the operator to include a message to the Yale Detachment in his "test." As a consequence, Barry was arrested as he stepped off the stagecoach two days later. It was probably the first time in B.C. that a policeman used the telegraph to catch a criminal. John Barry was convicted and hanged at Richfield. (See Heritage House book, *B.C. Provincial Police Stories: Volume One.*)

But the officers were not only on duty when the telegraph arrived but also the telephone and electric light, and when the four-horse stagecoach gave way to the train, the automobile and the airplane. As already mentioned, they were proud that their experiments enabled them to establish the first city-to-city short wave police radio communication system in North America.

Whether assisting victims of fire or flood, escorting fugitives from foreign countries, or merely performing the daily routine of urban duty, these British Columbia policemen did it with pride born of a sense of history. The Force was especially proud that apart from the initial appointment of Chartres Brew, every man who rose to top command began his career as a Constable. Among them was John H. Sullivan who had used the new telegraph line to prevent murderer John Barry from escaping justice.

In 1964 a few of the ex-policemen formed the B.C. Provincial Police Veterans' Association. Over 300 former policemen attended the First Annual Banquet, proving that while the Force was history, its spirit remained strong. Although Father Time is thinning the ranks, the Association is still active.

On behalf of the Association, I dedicate this book to the thousands of B.C. Provincial Policemen — the living and the dead — who for nearly a century served their province so well.

FOR THE FLYING DUTCHMAN — A HANGMAN'S NOOSE

In the blackness of the store one policeman lay dying, his unarmed companion fighting the most deadly duel in Western Canadian police history.

by Assistant Commissioner Cecil Clark

Quiet, methodical and absolutely fearless, Jack Russell joined the B.C. Police about 1912. After 35 years service, which took him criminal-chasing through the northern wilderness by snowshoe and dog team and along the southern coast by automobile, airplane and gas boat, he ultimately retired in Nanaimo as Inspector Jack Russell where he died at 73.

Jack spent his retirement fishing and hunting or tinkering with his power boat. He also had a small summer cottage on Gabriola Island where I spent a week with him.

In the summer evenings we'd sit out on one of the grassy head-lands overlooking the Strait of Georgia. On one of these evenings, watching the sun's dying light in the cloud-flecked sky above Comox, he dropped the name of the Flying Dutchman. Curious, I prodded his memory. He unfolded the dramatic story of the cat and mouse game the B.C. Police played along the Strait of Georgia's coastline in the early spring of 1913.

The Flying Dutchman's name was Henry Wagner. Had he been a peaceable citizen he'd probably have been dubbed "Dutch" Wagner, for he was born of German parents in Louisiana. But because he was a waterfront pirate who tore around the Strait of Georgia in the dark of the night, he got to be known as the Flying Dutchman.

The tempo of living on Vancouver Island in 1913 was just beginning to quicken. Automobiles had achieved self starters and electric lights, and were beginning to be seen more often outside city limits. Six Victoria firms were even using motor trucks, and one had been seen in Nanaimo. The vast Fraser River salmon fleet was still mainly sail propelled, but power boats were making an appearance, though still considered unreliable.

The small logging and fishing communities around the Strait were widely scattered. But any of importance had the standard wharf shed and float where it was the habit to leave freight and supplies uncollected for days at a time. Unfortunately, the march of progress was causing old-timers to shake their heads. Something was happening along the coast that year.

Henry Wagner, the Flying Dutchman.

Opposite: Constable Gordon Ross in later years when he was a detective on the Vancouver City Police Force.

The store where Constable Westaway was murdered and Ross captured the Flying Dutchman.

Nothing was safe anymore. Drums of oil, cases of kerosene, groceries and other supplies were being lifted overnight. Cottages and stores at lonely points were broken into. It looked as though the police would have to have something faster than their sailboats to check this modern trend.

The man then in charge of the up-Island B.C. Police was stockily built Chief Constable David Stephenson. From his office in the Nanaimo Courthouse, he kept an eye on the posts at Alberni, Comox, Cumberland and Union Bay.

After the first few reports about the depredations of the phantom night visitor, the conviction grew in Stephenson's mind that all these jobs were the work of one man with a fast boat — a novel way of operating in a era still dominated by sail. Here and there along the coast, when a store had been broken into at night, there were those who swore they heard the muffled throb of a fast engine over the water. Some, more motorwise than others, claimed they heard the rhythm of twin motors.

As the weeks developed, and the complaints continued, it was noticed that the phantom robber had struck twice at Union Bay, the coaling depot for coast shipping that lay between Nanaimo and Courtenay. Maybe the idea of "third time lucky" struck Stephenson. Anyway, he had a hunch that the Flying Dutchman would call there again. For one thing it was an important point on the highway, with Fraser & Bishop's Store and Post Office only 100 yards or so from the coaling docks.

Provincial Constable J. McKenzie, known to his intimates on the force as "Big Mac," was in charge at Union Bay. Although a capable man, he couldn't be everywhere and he certainly couldn't work night and day. Stephenson therefore assigned him two extra men, Gordon Ross and Harry Westaway, newcomers to the force.

Both were excellent physical specimens. Ross, a rugged Scot, had served in his teens in the South African war. Westaway, somewhat younger, was from Charlottetown, Prince Edward Island. Both men had joined the police the same day and were firm friends. After some probationary duty around Nanaimo, they were told to report to McKenzie. It was their first experience of police duty, and both were anxious to succeed.

Under McKenzie's direction they took up a night patrol, keeping as much out of sight as possible. They were told to pay special attention to the post office and store. It was a corner building with three entrances — a back door to the store, the main front entrance, and a side door into the post office.

Night after night Ross and Westaway prowled about, sometimes checking an incoming boat, every now and then returning to check the store, or they just stood unobserved in the gloom. Close to midnight on March 3, 1913, they were standing in the shadow of a clump of trees glancing up and down the deserted Island Highway, talking quietly. It had rained heavily earlier in the evening, and now the only sound was the occasional drip from the trees, or the vagrant, lonesome howl of a dog. Union Bay was asleep. But McKenzie was up and around, and had arranged to meet his assistants later.

Suddenly, Ross stiffened to attention. Then he grabbed Westaway's arm. "Look over there, Harry, a light, in the store!"

Sure enough, a flicker of light, a mere momentary gleam could be seen through the store's front window. Quickly the two officers covered the 200 yards to the building. For a surprise entry, they thought the best way was through the post office.

Quietly Ross applied his key to the lock and gently swung open the door. They entered and stood in the dark. By an oversight, Ross was unarmed but Westaway had a revolver. Ross, baton in one hand, flashlight in the other, took the lead and the pair tiptoed through the post office to the store entrance.

On the threshold Ross stood still and swept his flashlight beam across the shelves on the opposite side of the store. Then he swung it to the left, along the counter, behind the counter. Suddenly the light revealed a man's face, and, behind him, another man. The first was crouching on his right knee, and in his hand was a .44 revolver.

Ross instantly snapped off his flashlight and bounded toward the intruders. He had only taken a step when the store was rocked by the blast of the .44, the slug grazing Ross' shoulder then burying itself in Westaway's chest.

As Ross got his hands on the man with the gun, Westaway staggered back, sagged against the counter then fell to the floor. Before lapsing into unconsciousness he gave the hoarse advice, "Shoot him Gordon, shoot to kill — I can't help you."

At the blast of gunfire, the bandit's accomplice fled through the open back door. Ross, in the dark, didn't know of this development. All he knew was that he had his hands on one man and wasn't letting go.

Then, in the pitch black of Fraser & Bishop's Store, followed one of the greatest man-to-man battles in Western Police history — a groping, blind struggle for survival.

Both men were powerfully built, and to each it was a life and death struggle. The policeman knew the armed robber meant murder, and the desperado, thinking the policeman armed, knew he would use his gun if he could reach it. To Ross the one danger was that deadly .44. As he tried to wrench the revolver free, he heard Westaway groan in the darkness. But, engaged in his own titanic struggle, he couldn't help his companion. Then slowly, but perceptibly, he felt himself weakening as the bandit's fingers tightened round his windpipe. There was only one thought then in Ross' mind — stop that awful choking that was draining his consciousness.

Trying, in turn, to get his adversary's throat, the tough Scot succeeded only in getting his fingers in his opponent's mouth. Through his numbed arm he felt the stabbing shock that told him the teeth had bitten through to the bone.

Back and forth the deadly fight continued, the two desperately rolling over and over on the floor. Then the gunman got his gun free, and rained blow after blow on Ross' head. Blood-drenched and half blind, Ross managed to get out his baton and drove it viciously into the pit of his opponent's stomach.

The intruder collapsed on the floor, Ross astride him. Although both men seemed to be only semi-conscious after the fury of the struggle, Ross' Scottish tenacity spurred his dulled mind. One idea was uppermost — get the handcuffs on his man. They were the old fashioned, heavy Towers model, which often locked in a struggle. True to type, one of them locked, but Ross snapped the remaining open cuff on one of the desperado's wrists. Just then, with a sudden super-human heave, the prisoner on the floor rolled over and onto his knees, throwing Ross aside.

But the policeman still held the free handcuff. With his remaining strength he clubbed his baton down over the other's head, then again. With a grunt, the bloody prisoner collapsed on the floor.

Ross' scalp had been opened in a dozen places with the prisoner's gun butt, and in the dark, blood running into his eyes, he couldn't distinguish one wall from another. But he knew there was a window somewhere. Dragging the unconscious prisoner at the end of the handcuffs, he managed to find the window and smash it with his baton.

Twice he yelled for help. He thought he heard an answering yell. Then, through ears and his labored breathing, he heard another sound, a faint one from one corner of the store. It was Westaway. "Goodbye, Gordon, I'm going." It was his last utterance.

Meanwhile, Big Mac down near the coal dock thought he heard a shot in the village. He was on his way to investigate when the sound of a breaking window and a cry for help reached his ears. He made for Fraser & Bishop's Store. It was in darkness but he thought he saw figures inside.

Big Mac promptly put his shoulder to the locked front door. Inside, gun in hand, he snapped out a "Hand's up! Police!"

His flashlight picked out the details: a mess of broken shelving and overturned cases; a prone figure in one corner; a second sitting in another corner, one wrist shackled to a standing figure, so blood-covered and beaten that he was completely unrecognizable.

"Who are you?" barked McKenzie. Then it dawned on him.

The quickly summoned doctor signified that Westaway was beyond help. Ross and the prisoner were bandaged. An hour later Chief Constable Stephenson arrived from Cumberland with Constable Jack Russell.

As the stupified, bandaged prisoner lay on the steel slats of a cell bunk, Stephenson bent over and studied what was visible of his face. There was a big mole on the prisoner's right check. That settled things for Stephenson. Sharply, he demanded, "Who is your partner"

Through puffed and swollen lips came the answer, "Bill Julian."

It was enough. A listening Constable knew of Julian, a beach-comber who had a shack on Lasqueti Island.

Out of the cell, Stephenson's quick glance fixed on rookie Constable Ross. "You did a great job. You've caught the Flying Dutchman."

Stephenson went on to tell of word he had received from the State of Washington of Henry Wagner, alias the Flying Dutchman, who had done time in Walla Walla prison for shooting a sheriff, and was wanted for killing a postmaster. He was also credited with being a member of a gang of cattle rustlers, one of whom was Bill Julian.

For obvious reasons both fled the U.S., ending up on Vancouver Island. Here Wagner persuaded Julian to team up with him. Then the pair started their thieving spree in a fast boat. Not their own, of course, but one stolen from Puget Sound.

Less than an hour later, two Constables were headed in a power boat to Lasqueti Island. Circling to the far side, they anchored and crossed by trail to Julian's cabin. From a bush hideout late that afternoon they spotted a speck on the water which ultimately grew into a rowboat. They could see one man in it — a dispirited man, rowing listlessly.

As he landed the officers confronted him. There was, however, neither fight nor flight in Wagner's cattle rustling partner. Julian confessed to helping Wagner in several waterfront robberies, and in his shack were some of the proceeds.

Julian was obviously in fear of Wagner, and willing to tell all. He gave valuable evidence at Wagner's trial at Nanaimo, which got him off with a light five-year sentence for break and enter.

A grim-faced jury of Nanaimo miners convicted the Flying Dutchman of Westaway's murder. While he awaited execution, the ex-cattle rustler and water pirate was an unruly prisoner. Repeatedly attempting suicide, one morning he nearly succeeded in bashing his brains out on a radiator.

He claimed to the end that Ross didn't overcome him single-handed, and boasted he'd never been arrested by one man in his life. In a curious twist of bravado, he claimed there were two or three other policemen present that night in the Union Bay store. Unknown to him, however, he was fated to earn brief recognition by setting a new world's record.

On the morning of August 25, 1913, which, coincidentally, was Constable Gordon Ross' birthday, Wagner was escorted to a platform in the Nanaimo jail yard. Above the platform hung a noosed rope. The Flying Dutchman's murdering days ended abruptly.

It was a birthday that Constable Ross would never forget.

Two other men who also would never forget the date were B.C. police reporter B. A. McKelvie and Canada's official hangman, Arthur Ellis. He was attempting to set a new world's record for a speedy hanging and recruited McKelvie as a reluctant participant.

"It was a glorious morning," McKelvie was later to recall. "The sun was streaming into the dining-room of the Old Windsor Hotel at Nanaimo when I went down for an early breakfast. There was no one in the room as I entered. I was hardly seated when a dapper little man in a grey suit, with a pink rose in his buttonhole, bounced in and approached my table."

"May I sit here?" he questioned after giving me a cheery greeting.

"Certainly," I replied.

"You're up early this morning," he beamed.

I nodded agreement.

"Perhaps," he ventured, "you're going down to see the regrettable affair at the jail?"

"I am, unfortunately," I said.

"Ah, too bad that such things have to be," he murmured, shaking his head. "But then, men will commit crimes that the law decrees deserve capital punishment — and the law must be supported."

"I suppose so."

"Are you a commercial man?" queried my table companion.

"No, a newspaper reporter."

He fairly beamed. "Oh, I know a number of newspaper men," he volunteered.

From that introduction we drifted into a discussion of literature, and I found that the pleasant stranger was a great admirer of Browning. Suddenly he looked at his watch. "Oh," he explained, "I must be off." He bounced out of the room, turning at the door to smile, "I'll see you later."

When I stepped through the little door into the high-walled court-yard of the jail, to my surprise the first man I saw was my companion of the breakfast table. He rushed up to me. "You didn't know you had the honor of breakfasting with the public executioner," he said.

"I certainly did not!"

"Well," he chattered on without noting the chill in my reply, "I have a favor to ask of you."

I shuddered.

Arthur Ellis set a new world's record when he hanged the Flying Dutchman.

Police reporter Bruce McKelvie.

"This is the first time I have performed the execution of my duty on the Pacific Coast," he continued. "I find conditions here are identical with those under which my uncle established a world's record in executions in England in 1887. I'm out to establish a new world record. You see this Police Constable. He has a stop watch. I want you to stand beside him and see that the instant the condemned man's foot touches gravel when he comes through that door that the watch starts, and that it stops the second the trap is sprung."

The request was such a relief to what I expected he was going to ask me to do that I consented.

Then Arthur ran up on the scaffold. He faced the grim little crowd, rubbing his hands together and smiling agreeably. "Gentlemen," he said. "This is a wonderful country you have out here — and such glorious weather! This is the first time that I have visited you and as conditions are similar to those when my uncle established a world's record in executions, I am hoping to break that record today to celebrate the first time I have visited the Pacific Coast.

"Now, gentlemen," he said, growing serious, "when the condemned man appears you will kindly lift your hats — not necessarily out of respect for him, but for the law.

"Usually it is the custom to screen the foot of the scaffold so that you cannot see the condemned man after he disappears through the trap, but owing to the fact that this is my first time here and I am hoping to establish a new record, I have left the screen off, so you can see everything."

Just then the door opened. As the Flying Dutchman's foot touched the ground I saw the watch hand move. Accompanied by a Salvation Army officer and the Sheriff, he moved across the yard to the ramp that reached to the scaffold. I glanced at Arthur. He was crouched inward, a black cap in one hand and a leg strap in the other.

As they reached the trap, Arthur sprang into action. There was a black flash as the cap went on and, almost at the same time, the strap went about the Dutchman's legs. The Salvation Army officer had only time to murmur the first three or four words of the Lord's Prayer when the trap was sprung. Almost before the rope tightened, Arthur, with hand uplifted, shouted, "Time."

"Forty-seven seconds," answered the Constable, and he was correct.

"Gentlemen, gentlemen," beamed proud Arthur, again rubbing his hands, "you have been privileged to witness 11 seconds clipped from the record set by my uncle. You have seen a new world's record in hanging."

As for the Flying Dutchman, the other reluctant participant in the new world's record, he was beyond caring.

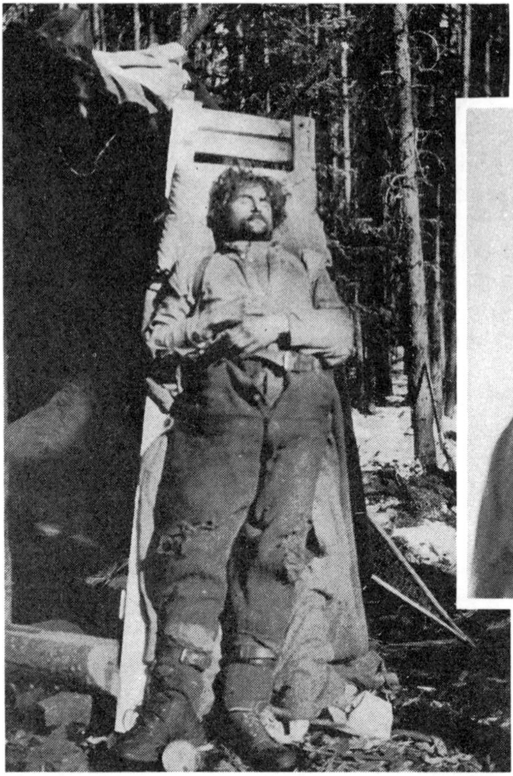

Crossing the Nechako River with the body on a sleigh. The poles carried by the two men are to help if they break through the ice.

Top left: The mad giant was killed in the shoot-out.

Top right: Constable F. F. O'Halloran who led the gruelling search for the mysterious and dangerous fugitive.

TRACKING THE NORTH'S MAD GIANT

The hairy figure roamed the wilderness of Central B.C., stealing from trappers and Indians, threatening anyone he met with his always ready rifle.

by Constable F. F. O'Halloran

I was a young Constable at Fort George (today's Prince George) when the mad giant started spreading terror in the district to the west. It was 1917, and many of the trappers and prospectors in the sparsely populated region had left their cabins to fight against the Germans in World War One. In early April, a dismal snowy season, first word was brought to us that the giant was hidden in the woods.

Bill Harper, a trapper, came in and reported being threatened by this unkempt figure. Bill said he met the giant as he was going along the trail. "The man," he said, "was well over six feet, bearded, and savage in appearance. He looked like a madman, dressed in rags and carried a big Winchester rifle of .45-90 calibre."

"I ran into him just by accident and he told me to turn around and go back the way I came. I didn't argue with him because I could see he had a bad look in his eye."

Chief Constable Minty asked Bill if he could locate the place where he had met the man. Bill could.

"Very well," said Minty, "will you go with O'Halloran and see if you can bring him in?"

We packed a lot of grub and, joined by Constable Charlie Evans, caught a freight train heading west. After we got off the train we had to hike about 35 miles through the bush to find the place where Bill had been intercepted.

It was tough going all the way. The bush was dense and the snow deep and soft. We finally arrived at the tent where the giant lived. He had the place barricaded so that he could hold off an army.

You could not creep up on him from behind. From the rear and from the sides he was protected, the only entrance being down a narrow gap toward the front of the tent. In addition, he had cut a hole in the canvas through which he could see everything approaching just as soon as there was any stir in the vicinity.

We edged in cautiously, for from Bill's description of the ruffian we knew we had to be mighty discreet. But when we arrived there the man was away. We entered the tent and it was the messiest place I have ever seen. There was a small stove, a couple of dirty blankets, a half-sack of horse oats and a frying pan.

I couldn't figure out how any man could have lived in such a hole and with no food in sight except the oats. While we were investigating, Bill and Charlie decided to explore the surrounding area.

I stayed in the tent and started a fire. After a while I began to feel uneasy. "Here you are," I said to myself, "all alone in a madman's tent. Your comrades are wandering in the bush and no doubt the madman is lurking around somewhere."

In all honesty I must admit I was slightly frightened. I got the fire going, picked up my rifle and started out in search of Bill and Charlie. I found them a little distance away and we compared notes. None of us had heard a thing, so we decided to return.

By this time it was snowing quite heavily — a soft wet snow that made the bush even more dreary than usual. The trail was bad and none of us felt any too cheerful about this assignment. But back in the tent we had a little food and made up our minds to stay for the night.

Suddenly, in the quiet of the night, came a tremendous racket. The next thing we knew the tent was smothering us and we were fighting to get free. The madman is back, I thought, as I struggled to get out from the folds of the tent. In a few moments we extricated ourselves and stood up in the darkness.

There was no madman. The heavy snow had been too much for the tent. The whole structure had collapsed. By now we were thoroughly disgusted, disheartened and discouraged. We decided that our man had left the country and that the wise move for us would be to go back and report to Chief Minty that the bird had flown.

So, about four a.m. in the dark, wild, wet morning we started hiking the 35 miles to the railroad track. That was the toughest trip I have ever been through. We sank deep into the snow with every step, we were all hungry, and over the entire district there seemed to brood the haunting spirit of the wild character for whom we were hunting.

Although I felt bad about giving up the chase, I figured the fellow had vanished and was miles away by now. We therefore had nothing to gain by waiting in his tent for him to return. Eventually we hit the railroad and caught the train for Fort George. On the train was a young Russian about 20 who got talking to us as people will in a pioneer country.

"You know," he told us, "I met a brute in the woods here the other day and I'm sure he is crazy. He is a regular giant. His face is covered with a black beard and he hasn't had his hair cut in years. His eyes are mad — the maddest eyes I have ever seen in a human.

"In fact, he doesn't look human. He's an animal."

He sounded like our man. We had a quick discussion, left the train and immediately started back to the tent, accompanied by the young Russian whom I had sworn in as a Special Constable.

We crossed the frozen Nechako River and slogged northward through the snow. That night we rested in a shack about 10 miles from the tent. We knew that the madman wandered from shack to shack in the district and we thought if he came to our shack we had better be prepared for him.

We placed a lot of newspapers around outside so that we would hear him approach. One of us kept watch, a huge club in hand, and the others tried to sleep. I couldn't rest. I kept tossing about on the cold floor, feeling that the giant was closer to us than we knew. Finally, about three a.m., we roused ourselves and decided to carry on to the tent. That was the most miserable morning I have experienced before or since.

As we trudged through the heavy snow and pitch black woods, none of us felt very happy. We knew that the madman was right at home in the woods. It would not have surprised us if he had suddenly started blasting at us from the darkness. All the while as we neared the tent I was turning over in my mind the possibility of smoking him out. He was armed and he was desperate. Not only was he not going to allow us to get too close, his barracades could have held off an army if he felt so inclined.

The low-hanging branches of the evergreens were loaded with wet snow and we had to feel our way along in the dismal gloom. We were wet, cold and hungry, and all of us felt dispirited. I was wishing I were back in the warmth of the Police Detachment and that the madman was somewhere on the China coast. But, we had a job to do. If we couldn't bring him in, then some other group would have to start all over again.

Before we arrived at the tent we stopped and made our plans, for we didn't want to take any chances.

"When we get there," I told the men, "we'll fan out around the tent. I'll take the front and call to him to come out in the name of the law ... and with his hands up.

"If he starts anything, and if he shoots at us, we'll throw a volley into the tent and smoke him out."

That plan agreed upon, we started forward once more. Presently, I knew we were close, and down through the gloom of the timber I could see the outline of the white tent. Creeping like shadows through the trees, the men spread out to cover the sides. I sneaked forward, dodging from tree to tree, until I figured I was close enough to make myself heard.

I can still remember that it was quiet as a tomb in the bush that dark morning. Not a leaf quivered, not a bird chirped in the whole expanse of timber. Then a very faint light started climbing in the east, lending ghostly shadows to the scene.

While we were getting into position the dawn had advanced until we could make out objects a considerable distance away. I kept my eye on the hole in the front of the tent. Such was my state of mind that I could swear a white eye gleamed madly at me through the torn flap.

When I saw that the boys were all in place, I ducked behind a tree for cover. We knew that our man was there for in the grey light we saw the tracks of his snowshoes in the new snow. In addition, one snowshoe was broken toward its end and we had heard that he travelled on a broken shoe. He was home, I was sure of that.

I looked to my rifle and saw that it was ready. I cleared my throat. As loud as I could shout I called, "Police! Hands up!"

The silence was intense, maddening. Not a move came from the tent, and I called again, "Police! Hands up!"

Then I detected a movement behind the canvas. I heard a wild roar, loud and wicked and full of fight. "Get to hell out of here!"

Immediately there was a sharp crack of a heavy rifle and I felt something smash against my face.

My God, I thought, I'm hit. I reached my hand up to wipe away the blood and I thought half of my head was gone. There was no blood. My face felt as if it were all there. I felt again and then I knew what had happened.

His bullet, directed toward the spot from where he had heard my voice, had torn away a huge hunk of bark from a tree alongside me. The bark had clipped across my check.

I raised my rifle. About the same time the other men fired a volley into the tent. There was deep silence.

I could see the other men standing in their positions behind the trees. I didn't move. I expected any moment to hear a shot from the tent and to see the wild man come charging into the open with blood in his eye.

For perhaps ten minutes we stood there and two or three times I called for him to come out with his hands up. There was no response. We gathered together, still keeping under cover and we discussed our plans.

"I have an idea he is just waiting for us to approach," Bill said. "You know how crazy men act. He is at this moment watching every move we make. The first man that draws near that tent is a dead duck."

I knew Bill was right. I knew the giant was not going to let us take him out. I'll have to admit that I had little stomach for the job ahead. But we couldn't just stand there all day while he had every advantage of us.

"I'm going in there," I told the group. "You fellows cover me as best you can. If I can draw him out, even to the door of the tent, you may have a chance to get him as he gets me.

"Keep your eyes on the flap and when it moves let him have it."

I left my rifle leaning against the tree and took my revolver in my right hand. Dodging from one tree to another, I sneaked closer and closer to the tent. I could feel my heart hammering and I knew that it was going to be a mighty close call.

Before the door of the tent he had built a log fence and he had the advantage of waiting until I tried to vault that fence. Then through the torn canvas he could riddle me.

The silence was the worst part. If he had been shouting at us I could have gone forward with much more courage. But there was something unearthly about the morning. The man was mad, no doubt, but he was also full of cunning. I came at last to the final barricade. Grasping the revolver tightly in my hand, I vaulted over.

As I landed on the other side, I stumbled slightly and lurched toward the tent. Working as fast as I could, I threw the flap open and pushed the revolver inside.

Then in the dim light I saw him — lying on his back on the floor. His huge frame almost filled the tent. His eyes were open, staring upward. He was dead as any man could be with a bullet through his heart.

My God, he was a sight!

His face was buried beneath a wild mess of black hair. His eyes were white, staring, wild. I thought, as I stood there looking at him, that he had eyes like a hawk. There was an almost inhuman expression in them.

His hair had not been cut or combed for years and it spread over his head like a mantle. He was clothed in rags, and lying by his side was the huge rifle which he always carried.

Bill, Charlie and the Russian came in answer to my call. We searched the tent and went through his pockets to uncover identification. All we could find in his ragged pockets was one American dime. There wasn't a note of any kind to give us a lead as to who he might have been. In the tent we found seven boxes of shells, and a number of boxes of matches which he had looted from cabins in the district.

Our work was finished for the moment. We threw his blanket over his huge body and started back. For awhile we debated the necessity for one of us standing on guard in case animals molested the corpse. But none of us wanted the job, so we risked leaving it alone until a party could be sent to remove the remains.

Later some Indians put the body on a sled and hauled it out for a coroner's inquest. They had a tough job, too, as the snow was melting and the river was slushy when they pulled the sled across.

Although the wild man was dead the mystery still remained about his identity. As the body lay in the funeral parlor in Fort George, trappers, bartenders, hunters, traders, prospectors and citizens were brought forward to view it. No one could identify the giant.

This situation was most unusual, for he had been a man standing six feet four inches and heavily built. He was not the type easily forgotten. After the body was shaved and cleaned up a number of people again looked at him but still there was no identification made. Chief Minty had some photographs taken and sent to police chiefs and sheriffs throughout Canada and the United States.

Some time later he received word from a sheriff in Montana. At last we had identified our man.

The sheriff told us that the giant had killed his partner five years earlier at Sweetgrass, Montana, and since that time had been the object of a police search. For five years he had lived like an animal in the woods around Fort George. He had felt, I believe, that every man was a policeman and that every man was a potential enemy.

He lived and ate just like a wild thing. No doubt the hardships he endured cracked his mind and drove him into the state in which we found him.

There were no roads since the community sat on a muskeg. I packed firewood — and everything else — up 58 steps to my house, and in the Detachment Office a stump protruded through the floor. It was life in

UNFORGETTABLE
PORT ESSINGTON

by 1st Class Constable Balfour E. "Bal" Munkley

(Port Essington dates back to the early 1870s when frontier trader Robert Cunningham pre-empted land on the south bank of the Skeena River some 12 miles from its mouth. He established a trading post and around it grew Port Essington, for a time probably the largest community north of Vancouver. From it sternwheel steamers plied 180 miles of the turbulent Skeena River to

Port Essington in the early 1900s when it was the largest community along the northern B.C. Coast. In the foreground and right center are salmon canneries, the fish boats dry on the tidal mud flat.

Opposite page, top: "Downtown" Port Essington in the early 1900s. Built on a muskeg, the community had no roads, although one of its many saloons did have the longest bar north of San Francisco.

In the early 1900s Port Essington was the supply center for not only the North Coast but also the Interior. From it sternwheelers such as the *Inlander* plied up the rock-strewn Skeena River 180 miles to Hazelton.

Hazelton, and around it many salmon canneries were established, two right in the community. Population reached several hundred with buildings that included a town hall, the north's first cold storage plant and, from time to time, four newspapers. However, with the completion in 1914 of the Grand Trunk Pacific Railway across Central B.C. to a new port called Prince Rupert, the community was bypassed. Today only rubble marks the site of the once flourishing coastal community.)

Port Essington Detachment was, to use a term more modern than the era of my story, "something else." I don't know what I did to deserve being stationed there, but in 1940 I was instructed to proceed to the one-man post from Terrace where I had married a local girl. I found out later that marrying a local girl almost automatically guaranteed a transfer.

Dorothy, my wife, and I packed and crated our worldly belongings and shipped them by the CNR to Prince Rupert where they were loaded on a small scow owned by the Donaldson brothers. Bright and early the following morning we boarded Donaldson's launch and, with our possessions in tow, arrived at our destination to find the house that was available to us. It was situated 56 steps up from the main boardwalk of the street. It wasn't a bad house and formerly had been the property of a cannery manager. One aspect of it was very satisfactory — the $4 a month rent.

Our first night was spent in the Port Essington Hotel which I am sure must have been the original building in town. We had an old iron bed in our room with a straw-filled pallet as a mattress, from which the straw kept falling out. The room was unheated and damned cold, and had no lock on its door. The following day I contacted the local magistrate who was also the postmaster, got the keys to the police office and the house, and with the assistance of our neighbors packed our goods up the 56 steps to our new home.

I learned from the magistrate that the population of Port Essington was largely made up of Indians, with a few whites and a few Japanese, and a few of origin that would be hard to define. My main job consisted of policing all the canneries scattered around the mouth of the Skeena River, among which were Oceanic, North Pacific, Sunnyside, and Cassiar. Access to Prince Rupert was either by boat direct or by the local ferry to Haysport, the CNR station across the river.

Port Essington had no paved or gravelled streets as it was sited on either rock or muskeg, and all thoroughfares were wooden planked. A large proportion of the buildings were supported over the river by pilings and one had to be careful when walking on some of the wharves and in other areas as the planking was nearing the half-century mark and had become rotten in some spots. A heavy person like myself learned to walk over the location of stringers.

The Skeena River at Essington had a very strong current notwithstanding it was very wide at that point. We were also located on tidewater and with tides in excess of 20 feet and with a flooding river it was no place for an amateur seaman. At low tide there was much exposure of stinking mud along the bank, and it certainly gave the community a distinctive air!

Our house had no electricity and was heated by wood-fueled fires. I found that the only way to obtain wood was to snag a log from the river and saw it. I was initially lucky as I was able to find a spruce log about two feet in diameter, and with a borrowed crosscut saw I bucked it into appropriate lengths on the river bank. Then I had to carry the blocks on a pack board up the 56 steps to the house. I counted those steps many times!

Although there was a store, we found it was much more satisfactory to order our groceries from Woodward's in Vancouver. The service provided by that company was terrific. I don't remember even an egg being broken. Each fragile item was wrapped and packed carefully at the same price of the goods in Vancouver. Our orders were shipped via Union Steamships and we paid the freight which was minimal. We figured we saved enough on our canned items alone to pay the transportation costs. Once a week I would be down at the dock meeting the *Cardena* with my hand cart to claim our provisions and carry the cartons up the 56 steps to where Dorothy and I would unpack them with the same eagerness as children opening Christmas presents.

There was not a great deal of crime for me to handle, although I had been warned that I should exercise caution at night. My predecessor had become involved in a brawl in the hours of darkness on the docks and had been pushed into the river. Fortunately, the tide was out and he was unhurt as he fell into the mud some 20 feet below. I discovered one night that the incident had created a lasting impression on my wife.

One evening about 10 o'clock, Dorothy and I were playing double patience (one of our million games) and I told her of my intention to make my usual patrol through the village to make sure all was secure. I said I wouldn't be long and would be back soon to join her in a cup of coffee. It was raining heavily as it often does in Port Essington. I patrolled the hotel area where I usually stopped for a word with the proprietor. The hotel had a beer parlor and only sold quarts which were shipped in wooden barrels. At that time it was illegal for Indians to consume or possess intoxicants. I was advised by the hotel keeper that there was a native dance in progress and some unsavory characters in the area as a result, no doubt to make a few dollars peddling liquor. By the time I thought things were quiet enough for me to go home it was almost 1 a.m. The rain was coming down in sheets and the night was as black as ebony with absolutely no lights.

I started to trudge my weary way home when I sensed that someone was approaching me in the dark. I paused until I was sure whoever it was was near and then triggered my flashlight. I saw a bedraggled figure wearing one of my slickers. It was my wife coming to look for me. I put my arm around her and she was trembling like a leaf. Under the slicker I felt the solid lump of an automatic pistol I had taught her to use proficiently. She could put eight shots into the silhouette of a man at 20 paces. She sobbed with relief on seeing me.

When I asked why she was out in the storm, she blurted, "Who the hell else would have come looking for you?" It was a very proud Constable who escorted his wife home that morning to a belated cup of coffee.

My office was a building that was part of the history of the community. It was situated about half a mile from our residence via boardwalks. The old record books were still there and I pored through them with interest. The structure was single-storey and consisted of a one-cell lockup and a small office. It had been built on piles over a swamp and they had settled, permitting a spruce stump to protrude into the middle of the office. No one in Port Essington seemed to think anything of a stump jutting through the floor, but visitors from "Outside" stared at it in amazement.

In the old days, a policeman was not given too much training before he was placed on duty. In my case, I had absolutely no training. The result was I learned by experience and listening to the advice of more knowledgeable persons. Therefore, it was often necessary for me to learn by trial and error as it were. I learned a lesson at Port Essington. Among other appointments I was ex-officio a Sanitary Inspector. There was a person employed by the Federal Government who insisted I do something about unsanitary conditions among many of the residents who did not have flush toilets. The category included most of the inhabitants. The complaint was that a number of outdoor toilets over the river bank were offensive. The fact that a good number of residents had no toilets at all at their homes and used those on the wharves, increased the complained-about conditions.

Accordingly, I armed myself with a quantity of Sanitary Inspection order forms and issued instructions to those householders who did not have toilets to remedy the situation "or else." Then I submitted a report to District Headquarters at Prince Rupert covering my actions.

A short time later I received a communication from Corporal Con Oland, a 30-year veteran. He put me on the right track. In his dry, humorous way he pointed out that my prowess as a Sanitary Inspector had resulted in the Commissioner having had new shoulder flashes made especially for me, consisting of an outdoor toilet with crossed dung forks. Then he added a P.S.: "Did you ever try to dig an outdoor toilet in a swamp?"

I got the message and made the rounds picking up the orders I had issued, advising their recipients to ignore them. They had fully intended to anyway!

He was chained, beaten and starved, but with kind
treatment he became a valuable and loyal companion.
I'll never forget

RINNY: MY FOUR-FOOTED POLICEMAN

by Corporal P. H. "Spike" Brown

Although Rinny, my German shepherd, was never gazetted as a member of the B.C. Provincial Police, he was nevertheless a valuable addition to the Force. The fact that his activities on behalf of law and order were cited a number of times in Crime Reports submitted by me and other officers entitles him to be remembered.

I acquired him by an unexpected circumstance when I was stationed at Cranbrook during the summer of 1932. On a late night patrol, Constable P. W. Jupp and I took into custody a German who was attempting to drive a dilapidated truck from Alberta to Vancouver

Cranbrook in the late 1930s.
Here Rinny became an
effective—although unofficial—
member of the Force.

without it being licensed, without his possessing a driver's license, without the vehicle having operating headlights, tail-light or trustworthy brakes, and without his having the sense not to drive while drunk. He had been travelling by night to avoid police scrutiny.

The offender was fined $50 and given the alternative of 30 days which he chose, and was placed in the city lockup. Chained to his belongings on the truck was a dog, a youngish animal though full grown, half-starved and obviously mistreated. He was also vicious, not surprising considering his past treatment and that he was in unfamiliar surroundings and separated from his master, even though the man did not deserve his loyalty.

At the trial of the German, Stipendiary Magistrate John Leask enquired as to the disposition of the dog while its owner was in jail. Being single, I volunteered to look after him. The dog's name was Rinny, short version of Rin Tin Tin, named after the dog of movie fame.

He fought ferociously when I moved him from the truck to chain him to a post in the yard behind the Detachment Office which was on the ground floor of City Hall where I occupied a bedroom. Then he

The author, second from right, forms part of the Guard of Honor at the funeral of Commissioner John H. McMullin on May 11, 1943.

40

would not allow anyone to approach him. I made sure he received food and water from me alone, but it was still a week before he would permit me to place a hand on him. In the meantime, the jailed owner made a proposition. If I would pay his fine I could keep the dog as security, and he would claim him later. I agreed, thinking he would not return. On his release the man obtained a temporary job and earned enough to legalize the operation of the truck and have it repaired. Then he went on his way to Vancouver.

I proceeded to gain Rinny's confidence, feeding him myself and currying his unkempt coat until it was glossy. I found he had been beaten unmercifully, quite likely many times, as he had scars to show for it. Gradually the outlines of his ribs disappeared as he gained weight, and gradually, too, he accepted me as his master. He insisted on lying at the foot of my bed when I slept and accompanying me on pedestrian patrols of the city.

He was a most intelligent animal and had been trained to perform many tricks. His owner had used him as a one-feature circus from town to town in order to pick up donations from spectators to finance his trip to the Coast. Although he had been trained in German, Rinny was knowing enough to understand what I wished him to do when I instructed him in English. He learned to ascend a ladder to the roof of a building and descend by the same means. The proprietor of the store where Jupp and I had a newspaper reserved for us soon knew what to expect. Rinny, when ordered to fetch the paper, would trot through town and return carrying the rolled news in his mouth. How he avoided wetting it with his saliva or imprinting it with his teeth, I do not know, but he always delivered it in good condition.

With the care he received, Rinny's disposition quickly changed. He was no longer the savage animal that had come to the Detachment. He soon learned to recognize the police uniform and was always friendly to its wearers. But he had a sense of who were prisoners, and took it upon himself to guard such persons when they were brought to the lockup or had to be removed from it for any reason. He made sure they knew he was close by, warning them with a growl and show of teeth if he suspected they were the least out of line in their actions. He was so efficient that Jupp and I and the other officers who were handling prisoners came to thoroughly rely upon his vigilance, even though we had temporarily to absent ourselves and leave him in charge. Perhaps it wasn't according to regulations, but it worked.

He was almost as good as a third man when Jupp and I were on patrol of streets and alleys. He would choose an area we had not as yet covered and patrol it on his own, bringing our attention to anything he felt unusual by a series of wolf-like howls. He found many a passed-out drunk, and perhaps in the winter saved some of their lives for it can be bitterly cold in Cranbrook.

He seemed to have an uncanny instinct of things being wrong. One of his accomplishments was to test rear doors of shops and other premises at night by throwing his weight against them. If he found them insecure, he came in search of Jupp or me and led us to the scene.

We came to know it was unwise to ignore him when he indicated he wished us to follow for he always had a worthy reason.

Late one Saturday night I was on patrol alone and observed an inebriated man shouting obscenities at passersby, many of them women and girls on their way home from the movie. I overtook him, but as he promised to go to his room in a nearby hotel I sent him on his way with a warning. Not long after I found him causing a disturbance in the Golden Pheasant Cafe so I decided to lock him up. Rather than parade him through the Saturday night crowd on Baker, the main street, I took him down back alleys. He was a great hulk of a man, but came with me meekly until we were part way down the first lane. Here we came to some tools the city road repair gang had carelessly left. Among them was an extra-long crowbar. My drunk made a lunge for it and came at me whirling it in circles of such circumference I could not get near him.

Knowing that I stood a good chance of having my skull crushed if he connected, I was dodging and ducking in efforts to seize him, but getting nowhere. Just then I saw Rinny's silhouette at the end of the alley in the course of one of his patrols. Even before I could shout to him, he came bounding and hurled himself at my assailant's back, knocking him sprawling.

With Rinny snarling over the now terror-stricken man, I was able to handcuff him. Then, with him too frightened of my fellow "patrolman" to walk properly, I half dragged him to the lockup. In the morning we learned our prisoner was Rusty Davidson, wanted in Nelson for safe-cracking. That was one time Rinny's "policing" was mentioned in a Crime Report. Jupp and I saw to that, and also to him receiving a huge steak and several delectable bones as a reward. (Steak was about 25 cents a pound in those days.)

Another time I was alone in the Cranbrook office at night doing paper work. Rinny was lying on the floor by the desk as was his habit when I attended to such chores. I had previously locked the prisoners in their cells, noticing that the door to the toilet off the bull pen (main room of the cell block) was closed. I thought nothing of it since it was often closed after one of our enforced boarders used the facility. Rinny kept pricking up his ears as though listening and had gone several times to the outer door of the cell room and whined. Finally, he took the flare of my breeches in his teeth and tugged me to the door.

Puzzled, I entered the lockup but could find nothing amiss until Rinny pawed at the closed toilet door. When I opened it there was the sound of water trickling from the tank above the bowl. I found it was caused by part of the plunger's wire having been removed. As well I found one of the bars of the toilet room window partially cut through. I called Jupp. He came from his home and we searched the cell block.

We found the missing wire honed to a needle point and useable as a weapon as deadly as an ice pick, and several hacksaw blades, all secreted above a hot-water radiator which hung from the ceiling. Rinny's sense of something wrong was right again. But how he knew it was necessary to investigate is a mystery to me.

On another occasion in Cranbrook we had to arrest a young Indian who had hidden in the basement of his girl friend's home where she and others of her family were under quarantine because of an infectious disease. Fire Chief Adams, who was also the city's health officer and who was with us, prepared to place our man in hospital under police guard until it could be proven he was free from contamination. None of us, however, was inclined to enter the premises because of the quarantine. Rinny became impatient with the inaction, leaped through a glassless basement window and brought our intended prisoner out.

Much to my surprise Rinny's owner did return to claim him, and I was obligated to turn him over. But the dog had ideas of his own. When he saw his former master he went for him with bared fangs. If I had not held him by his collar I am sure he would have injured the man most severely — perhaps killed him. The man made a hasty retreat and that was the last we ever saw of him.

When I was transferred to Penticton and was on night duty there for the first time, Rinny was doing his alley patrol and came across a man climbing through the rear window of a shop. His howls brought me on the run to discover that the apparent prowler, beside himself with fear as Rinny snarled at his feet, was a baker who had forgotten his key. He had pried up the window to gain entrance to his own place of business. That incident for Rinny and me proved very rewarding. We were always assured of a large slab of fresh, hot bread dripping with butter and smeared thickly with jam at any time around dawn of a winter morning when the loaves came out of the oven. In addition, there was a mug of hot coffee for me and a bowl of milk for my four-footed patrol mate.

It was in Penticton that I met the girl who later became my wife. She was an operator at the telephone exchange. When both of our shifts ended at midnight I would call for her and walk her home. Rinny would accompany us. When my shift changed and I couldn't escort my lady home Rinny was worried. He could see her walking off by herself without me and decided if I wouldn't, or couldn't, see her safely home, he would. When he had completed his self-elected duty he would return to the Detachment and if I was away seek me out and go about his police routines. She told me twice that when Rinny was with her she had been bothered by louts, but he had sent them scurrying.

From Penticton I was posted to Powell River where Rinny ensconced himself as a member of that Detachment. He faithfully patrolled alleys as before, all except one which a large half-wild female warehouse cat made her stamping ground. He had an encounter when she had dropped on his back from a shed roof when he got too close to her kittens, and had dug her claws into his hide. Henceforth he gave that alley a wide berth.

When I moved to North Vancouver Rinny was as diligent a policeman as he had been elsewhere, and when I was transferred to Agassiz he was equally efficient. One night Constable Jack Blezard and I had to attend to a complaint originating at the Scowlitz Indian

Reservation about 11 miles away. We decided, as we knew Rinny disliked Indians, to leave him secured by his leash to one of the verandah railings of the house my wife and I rented.

Jack and I had to pass my home and we thought Rinny would not notice the police car as we were travelling after dark. If he did, he would not suspect my presence if I ducked out of sight. Eleven miles from Agassiz we found an automobile abandoned by the roadside, left our car to check it, then proceeded to the Reserve.

On our return, Rinny was circling the vehicle we had inspected. He could scent us, but had not as yet decided which direction we had gone. Like a war-horse hearing the bugle, he had been alerted by the police car passing my residence, and in spite of my hiding had somehow known I was in it. He had vaulted the porch railing, ripping out the small upright to which his leash was fastened. Dragging it, he had run over the 11 miles of rough, gravelled road. He was in a lather when we found him, his paws bleeding from the sharp stones he had travelled over, and thoroughly exhausted. We placed him in the rear of the car and took him home, but he was so exhausted that it was several days before he was normal.

From Agassiz he went with me to Victoria and there he became a problem. Accustomed to his freedom in roaming small towns and villages, he could not understand why it was not permissable for him to accompany me to the office which was a considerable distance from where my wife and I lived. He would break loose and set off in search of me. A number of times I had to phone my wife to come and take him home when he arrived early in the day at the office.

Rinny's roaming became dangerous for him. He would reach the office and if I had walked into downtown Victoria, he would trail me, only to become confused by the much heavier traffic than he had known in other Detachment areas. The city police repeatedly found him cowering in fright in front of streetcars and impeding their progress, and took him to their headquarters. They knew he was mine by the identification on his collar which included one of our uniform lapel badges.

When he could not trail me by scent from the office, his dilemma was worse, and he would range all over the city. Finally, I decided something had to be done for his safety for I was always in fear of him being struck by a car. With a heavy heart, I gave him to a Victoria City Policeman who had a small farm in Saanich and who promised to give him a good home. He had children, and since Rinny loved children I knew he would be happy with them. I checked several times with my police friend and learned that my old patrol buddy had, after a period of fretting, settled down in his new environment and seemed content. It was there he ended his days.

Constable George Cassidy, left, lived to be nearly 100.

A police Guard of Honor at his funeral in 1948.

One of the most unusual — and
potentially tragic — incidents in the long history of the
B.C. Provincial Police was

THE KILLER FROM IOWA

by Deputy Commissioner Cecil Clark

The vagaries of chance occasionally play an important part in everyone's life. Never was this statement more true than in the case of Charles Jones who in 1909 was living at Ladysmith on Vancouver Island, or George Cassidy who was the Provincial Police Officer in the community.

In fact, only by chance did George survive to become a policeman. He was born in Ireland in 1848, the year of the potato famine. It was a time of misery that saw a million of his countrymen die of virtual starvation in the following decade, and another 1.5 million emigrate to the New World.

But survive he did. At 21, he landed in New York. Five years later he was one of some 80 teamsters freighting supplies for General Terry's army then invading the wild Black Hills of Dakota. As the blue-clad cavalry, including General George Armstrong Custer, pushed the warlike Indians before them, 15,000 gold-hungry miners followed to establish such rip-roaring frontier communities as Deadwood and others where the law of the six-shooter prevailed.

In this brawling life and death atmosphere Cassidy came to know Wild Bill Hickok and Calamity Jane, though chance decreed that he

45

would escape the flying lead that occasionally formed part of Deadwood's night life. The following year, when he was slated to move further west with Custer's cavalry, chance again took a hand. Cassidy, on a whim, decided to go to California. For this reason a year later he read of the massacre of Custer and of his troopers instead of being part of it.

From California in 1879 the wandering George came to B.C., mainly to see his cousin Tom Cassidy, a Vancouver Island farmer. Then in 1895, George Cassidy joined the B.C. Provincial Police. One of the places he was stationed was Ladysmith on Vancouver Island, and here he encountered the strangest example of chance that a man is likely to experience.

At the time the community relied on coal mining for its existence, some 2,000 of the male population working underground. One of them was Charlie Jones, a bachelor who had drifted into town the previous fall. For a time he worked as a bartender in a Ladysmith saloon, until finally he got a job as a mule-driver in No. 4 Mine at Extension.

A quiet-spoken man in his early 30s, Charlie had a room in town where he lived alone, saying little about his affairs and practically nothing about his past. He didn't gamble or drink and his presence in the community went unnoticed until the evening of June 23. Then an American Negro called Brown noticed him. What he saw was a man wanted for a five-year-old murder in the State of Iowa.

Hurrying down to the Provincial Police Office, Brown unburdened himself of his news to Constable George Cassidy. He was positive in his identification, describing how Jones had been a bartender in the coal mining town of Albia in southern Iowa. Then he was known as Charlie James who, in December 1904, shot and killed a man in a barroom argument. Then he disappeared.

Brown had more than passing interest in finding the fugitive. The day when he left Albia to see the West, the Sheriff of Munroe County promised him $200 if, in his travels, he ran on to the trail of Charlie James. So positive was Brown in his statements that Cassidy interrogated mule-skinner Jones. In his usual quiet way he denied that he was the wanted man and said that he'd never been in Iowa in his life.

Nevertheless, there in the background was the accusing Brown. Cassidy passed word to his District Chief and in turn the Victoria Headquarters wired Iowa. Back came a prompt reply that the Albia killer was still at large — and his description completely fitted the Ladysmith suspect. Charlie was arrested and taken to Victoria's Hillside Avenue Jail to await an escort from Iowa.

When word of the arrest spread around Ladysmith it temporarily diverted discussion from the advent of sewers and electric light, a civic step proposed for that fall. A good many took the part of Charlie Jones, claiming that it was possibly a case of mistaken identity. They just couldn't believe that Charlie was the sort of man who could be associated with a killing.

Three weeks went by. Then there arrived from Seattle Sheriff W. B. Griffin from Iowa, along with Dr. Hyatt, the coroner who performed the autopsy on Charlie James' alleged victim, and H. A. Armstrong. All three had been sufficiently acquainted with the killer to make identification possible.

Charlie Jones was brought out to confront the trio, each of whom promptly identified him as the fugitive murderer. Jones merely regarded his accusers with an unbelieving smile and said nothing in his own behalf.

Later that day Sheriff Griffin told Superintendent Hussey of the B.C. Police that after the Christmas killing, James had vanished in a somewhat mysterious manner. Rumor was that he had later taken a train out of town disguised as a woman. A sheriff's deputy who checked the railway station after the killing had noticed that the only person in the waiting room was a woman engrossed in a book. They felt the lone woman must have been the killer, James.

James, if he was James, waived extradition but before he was taken to the Seattle steamer asked one favor. He wanted to make a phone call to Ladysmith. It was to a girl, and though her name was never released, apparently she had complete faith in the innocence of Charlie Jones. Charlie vowed to her that he was innocent, that he would soon be back and then they would get married.

By now Ladysmith gossip, with the news of the positive identification in Victoria, had turned against Jones. People began to recollect his strange silences on the subject of his past history, certain evasions in his conversation. Then came news that Constable Cassidy had found a loaded revolver among the suspect's effects in a local boarding house. A month later came news of an extraordinary climax to the story.

When other accusers faced Jones in Albia, some of them weren't so sure that he was the right man. One or two, in fact, were absolutely positive he wasn't! Suddenly, while these conflicting opinions were being aired, chance took another turn. To the astonishment of everyone in Ladysmith came word that the real murderer had been caught.

When he was returned to Albia the real James turned out to be a man so like Jones in appearance that he was almost a double. The only difference was that, unlike Jones, he carried a burden of guilt and confessed to the killing.

Whether Charlie Jones hastened back to Ladysmith to marry the girl who so staunchly believed in him is something research doesn't disclose. It would have been a satisfactory conclusion to one of the most extraordinary stories of how blind chance twice played an incredible part in a man's life.

George Cassidy, the man who'd known Deadwood City and the warring Sioux, whose escape from the Custer massacre was in itself a bit of blind chance, retired from the B.C. Provincial Police in 1913 after 18 years' service. He died in 1948, a few months short of his 100th birthday. It is safe to say that in his colorful career he could point to no stranger case of chance or coincidence than the story of Charlie Jones.

POLICEMAN'S WIFE ON THE FRONTIER

She was four months by saddle horse and dog team in sub-zero weather reaching the shack that would be home, the nearest community 250 roadless miles away, and she was alone for weeks while her husband was on patrol in the vast surrounding wilderness.

by Sergeant C. G. Barber, as told to G. M. Rutherford

It was -30°F and a searing wind swept the frozen country outside the log cabin. An uninviting prospect, but Sergeant Barber glanced from the window and commented in a matter-of-fact tone, "Not so bad. If it stays like this, I'll be back inside three weeks."

His wife, getting up from the breakfast table, observed quietly, "If you are, it will be the first time since we've been here."

The setting was Fort Nelson in remote northeastern B.C. It was a multi-thousand square-mile expanse of trees, the only whites a few fur traders and trappers. The nearest white habitation was Fort St. John some 250 wilderness miles to the southward, the nearest railroad some 600 miles away at Prince George in Central B.C. Sergeant C. G. Barber had come in the year before, 1926, to open the Detachment, and his wife, Hanna, had come too. It had begun with a call from the Inspector to Fort St. John.

"On the strength of your previous patrols into the Fort Nelson area," he said, "I think you are the man to go in and open the new Detachment there. I believe you said there was a cabin that could be used?"

"Yes, it was in sound condition last time I saw it," the Sergeant replied. "My wife would go in with me." he added.

"Well, that is up to you of course. Much nicer for you if she can stand it. Should be all right having a cabin to go to. How long do you think it will take to get there?"

"About three months, I should think, we'll have so much to take in with us."

"Well, that's settled then," the Inspector said. "Make your own arrangements."

They left Fort St. John on September 22. For over four long months of cold and a tent for shelter, the Sergeant's wife travelled by horseback, then when snow arrived, strapped to a swaying dog sled. She ached all over from the forced position, until in her thoughts the

---

Opposite page, left to right: Chief Bigfoot, Chief Fantas whom Barber later found starving and abandoned by his tribe, Sergeant Barber, interpreter, and Chief Bellyful.

Mrs. Barber bidding goodbye to her husband and Constable Forfar as they left Fort St. John on their exploration trip to Fort Nelson.

In 1923 Constable Barber, far left, and Constable Forfar pioneered a route from Fort St. John to Fort Nelson through more than 250 miles of wilderness. For the first 20 days they averaged only 10 miles a day. Some 20 years later the Alaska Highway followed their route for 200 of the 250 miles between Fort St. John and Fort Nelson.

desolate little cabin ahead became the promise of all her desires, with warmth and space to move more freely.

The end of the journey came at last on January 18. She was probably the first white woman over the Arctic watershed in B.C. As they came in sight of the cabin that was to be their home for two years, her heart sank. It was so weatherbeaten and forlorn. Her husband swore as he saw the log building closely for the first time since his last patrol eight months ago.

"The chinking is mostly out," he said bluntly, "it won't look much like home inside."

He and one of the drivers managed to get the door open. Then they stood for a moment looking in despair at the desolation inside. Snow, driven between the logs where the chinking had fallen out, lay in every corner, with drifts piled up against the rough table and chairs. Overcome with disappointment and weariness, Hanna leaned against him and wept.

But now they had been at the Post a year, and the cabin had been transformed. It had a warm and homelike air, and the Sergeant was just preparing to leave on a patrol. His wife faced the weeks of solitude ahead calmly. Sam, an elderly Indian, would come and see every second day about her wood and other chores. Apart from him she was alone and out of touch except for chance callers wanting to see the policeman. They were her real fear, though her husband only half guessed the moments of sheer dread that accompanied a knocking on the door after dark.

She put these thoughts aside and checked his pack and supplies. She could think of nothing missing, and the dogs were ready to go. "There," she said, "and if you're a day over three weeks I'll go home to mother." The impossibility of the joke brought a lump to her throat, and she pushed him hastily out of the door.

Sergeant Barber travelled all day, with one short stop for food, and as afternoon drew in he arrived at the cabin of Goddard, a trapper who had lodged a complaint against a man named Thompson for stealing pelts from him. The wind was sharper now as he breasted the last rise and saw the smoke from Goddard's chimney. He realized that he was cold and hungry, and thoughts of a hot meal spurred him on.

"Hello there, Sergeant, I expected you'd be along one day soon," said a stocky, bearded man who answered his call. Heat and the savory smell of food poured out of the partly open door. "You're just in time. The wind's rising."

Barber stayed the night, and they arranged to go together and see Thompson next day. The same icy wind with the thermometer still hovering around -30°F faced them when they left in the morning. They found their man at his shack. After a good deal of hedging and lying, he admitted taking the pelts and selling them. He pulled a bag of money from a loose board in the floor and offered to pay Goddard back what he had received for them.

"That's all right with me," Goddard replied.

"If you're both satisfied we'll leave it at that this time. Anything of the sort again, Thompson, and you'll be on the inside looking out," the Sergeant warned.

That settled, he left to continue his patrol.

It was nearly mid-day and a bright, hard sun glittered on the stretches of snow. The Sergeant had been wondering whether there was any chance that his friend Bob Lock would turn up at home while he was away. If he did, he would probably take Hanna over to the Hudson's Bay Post on the mouth of the Fantas River. It was a long day's trip, but Lock's wife was there and always enjoyed the rare visits. Bob Lock was an Englishman, trapping for a living, and Mrs. Lock was the only female acquaintance Hanna could speak to in that womanless country.

The trackless snow swept away on every side, broken only by scattered growths of scrubby fir along the frozen Fantas River. Up ahead he could see a bend in the river and a wide belt of trees where a fire had burned through, leaving the poplar dead but standing. A little further up he knew there was a Fantas Indian encampment. The chief was very old, and it was said he remembered when the original Fort on the Nelson River was burned down in the 1830s. The Sergeant made his way through the fire-killed poplar, but stopped abruptly as he heard a wavering call. "Mit-soo-ule."

The call came again in a weak, trembling woman's voice: "Mit-soo-ule."

"Food all gone," he interpreted to himself. Then he saw her. An old squaw bent and hunched, her color matching the brown dying poplar about her. His knowledge of the Indian language was sketchy, but it satisfied the occasion.

"Where you come from?" he asked.

She pointed back into the trees and beckoned him to follow.

"She must be very old," he thought as the little wizened figure limped and struggled along ahead of him. A thin wisp of smoke and the squaw pointed eagerly. They had arrived.

For a moment Sergeant Barber was speechless, and stood simply staring. In the little clearing was an Indian wickie-up. It was shaped like a pup tent and made of brush piled on thickly about three-quarters of the way up, the top open to let out the smoke. In front of this sat an old Indian, his head sunk on his bare chest and his coarse grey hair, tied with a now colorless ribbon, hung over his shoulders. He wore only a breech clout and a pair of moccasins to keep the penetrating cold from his ancient frame. As they came into the clearing he raised his head and the Sergeant saw that he was blind. An old, old man, his fine high cheek bones and aquiline nose speaking of a past vigor that his starved body could no longer imitate.

"What tribe?" the policeman asked.

"He Chief Fantas," the squaw told him. She put her hands to her eyes and then to her ears, shaking her head and pointing at the emaciated figure by the wickie-up.

The Chief, past his usefulness, had been discarded — deaf and blind. Anger and pity overcame the white man. He cursed the younger

Indians who had put the old couple there to die now that they were too old to hunt.

"He Chief Fantas," the squaw said again. She went to him, taking his hand and putting one finger up to tell him one man was there. He nodded his head.

"Mit-soo-ule," he said.

"No food at all?" the Sergeant asked.

The old woman shook her head. She waved a hand towards some small poplars that had been cut down, then to the fire, shrugging her shoulders and uttering short gutteral sentences between each movement.

Hardly any wood either, apparently. A rope was tied from the wickie-up to a tree, and then further on to another. In this way the old Indian had felt his way out and chopped the wood for their fire. He would have to take a chip off the bark with his axe and smell it to see whether it was green or dead. Then, finding a dead one, hack away at it, his feeble strokes making a long job of the poplar which would be about eight inches in diameter at the butt. After it fell it still had to be cut into 20- or 25-foot lengths and dragged back to the wickie-up.

The squaw's despairing gestures expressed plainly how the work was too much for him now, and the wood he had stacked a few months ago was almost gone. Their plight was desperate. Old, ill and alone, without food or wood, they would soon have died had the squaw not seen him.

Stooping low and stepping round the fire, which burned dully, Sergeant Barber entered the wickie-up. The fire was in the centre and the lengths of poplar went right through and out at the ends, which were open. When the logs burned away in the middle, the ends were drawn together from both sides.

To the white man it seemed just as cold inside as out. He looked in admiration at the extraordinary figure of old Chief Fantas, said to be 100 years old, clothed simply in a hair ribbon, a breech clout and a pair of moccasins in a temperature of -30°F. The squaw evidently spoke the truth when she said mit-soo-ule. Sergeant Barber could find nothing in that bare place except for two teaspoonsful of grey-green flour in a tin.

In the old days it was customary for the Indians to get rid of their old people by abandoning them. But now the practice was forbidden and the police had authority to issue rations to Indians too feeble to hunt.

"I get some food back in two days," he told the squaw, and left them some biscuits from his own supply until he returned.

On patrols of that huge Fort Nelson area, he covered between 1,200 and 1,400 miles during the winter months, a round-trip taking weeks of steady travelling. Completely at home in his vast northern Detachment, he headed straight for the Hudson's Bay Trading Post at the mouth of the Fantas River. He arrived there the next day.

"Hello, Sergeant, who are you after?" they greeted him.

"No one this time, just supplies," he laughed. "I found Chief Fantas and his squaw out in a wickie-up, no food and in a bad way."

"I heard they had a new Chief. So that is what they did with the old boy. Rather a tough life when you are a hundred. His squaw is no chicken, either; somewhere in the nineties, I guess," the trader said. "He must be the last of the chiefs of pre-white man days around here, almost worth preserving."

"That is what I'm trying to do," the Sergeant replied dryly. "Here is the order: 24-pound sack of flour, five pounds of bacon, one-half pound of tea, three plugs of tobacco. Let's see now, as it's nearly Christmas, how about a two-pound can of syrup and some baking powder. That'll do for now, but I want you to supply them with enough rations to keep them going. They're about a mile below the Indian encampment on the river."

"They'll go crazy with joy," the trader predicted. "By the way, your wife is here. Bob Lock brought her in the day before yesterday. Haven't seen her for six months. She certainly looks fine; one of the few women that can stand this life."

"She's here? Well, that is a bit of luck. I'll take the stuff and get over there."

"Now for a surprise," he thought as he made for Lock's cabin. The dogs seemed to know that it was the last lap before feeding time, and the short distance melted under their eager feet. The amazement of his wife and friends when they saw him arrive was just as he had expected. After he explained the reason for his unscheduled call at the Hudson's Bay Post, Hanna commented, "So, you wouldn't have been home in three weeks after all!"

Next day Hanna and Bob Lock decided to go back with him and see the wickie-up. They set off in the early morning and arrived in the afternoon. The Chief's wife had heard them coming and was pulling her husband outside.

The Sergeant unstrapped the provisions and gave her each thing separately. She prodded and turned the item, then passed it to the old man. He felt it carefully and smelled it to be quite sure, then said, "Marci, marci" — thank you, thank you —, his face wreathed in smiles.

The only remaining job to do for the Chief and his wife was to make some arrangement about their wood, so the Sergeant went to the Fantas encampment a mile away. He got a number of young Indians to go into the woods near the wickie-up and cut enough dry poplar to last until spring.

With this problem taken care of, the policeman resumed his journey. For Sergeant Barber it had been a routine patrol — days alone in sub-zero weather, his dogs for company and only his own knowledge between him and disaster.

For his English-born wife it also had been routine. Days alone in a cabin with a bucket for water, outhouse behind the cabin, coal-oil lamp to penetrate the long, long Northern nights, the nearest white woman a long day's travel by dogsled. Above all, there was the always present concern for her husband, patrolling alone in the harsh unexplored country where the temperature could drop to -50° F, and a blizzard last for days. No way to inform anyone if he met with an accident and always the danger that he could disappear without trace as had many other wilderness travellers.

Why did she choose such a life? Perhaps only another policeman's wife could know. The following tribute to Hanna Barber was written by Mrs. G. M. Thomson, whose husband was a Provincial Policeman at Kamloops:

A LOVELY LADY

One day I saw a picture
Of a sweet little English bride.
Her husband stood beside her
In all his manly pride.

She was lovely, gentle, and trusting
But little did she know
Of the future in store, on Canadian shores
Or of life in the Arctic snow.

Her husband became a policeman,
Was sent away up North
Where any man, who is a man,
Will prove what he is worth.

His little wife went with him,
Up to the frozen snows
As a lawman's bride, she stayed by his side,
That was the life she chose.

She's sat alone in their cabin at night
Unafraid, but wondering when
Through the long hard days in the Northland
She would see her husband again.

She's stood by the bed of sick ones,
Easing their anguish and pain,
And when he returned from his journeys
Knew it was not in vain.

She's been with her man, thru' the great Alcan,
When 'twas nothing but wilderness there,
She speaks with pride, of the man at her side
And the hardships they had to share.

They left the Northland together,
That country of dog-team and snows,
The hardships, treks, and bad weather
The wife of that lawman knows.

Who is this gracious lady?
The beloved of all the force,
The Inspector's devoted "Little Un,"
Why, it's Mrs. Barber, of course!

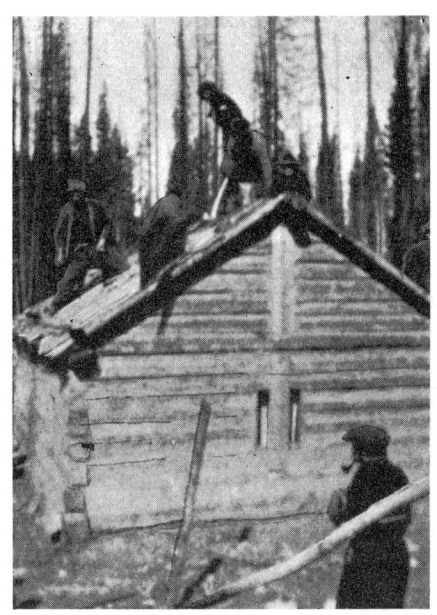

Mrs. Barber's "dream home" at Fort Nelson turned out to be an abandoned log shack. Mail came regularly — about every four months.

When Sergeant Barber retired as an Inspector in 1946, one of his Detachment members wrote and illustrated the following tribute:

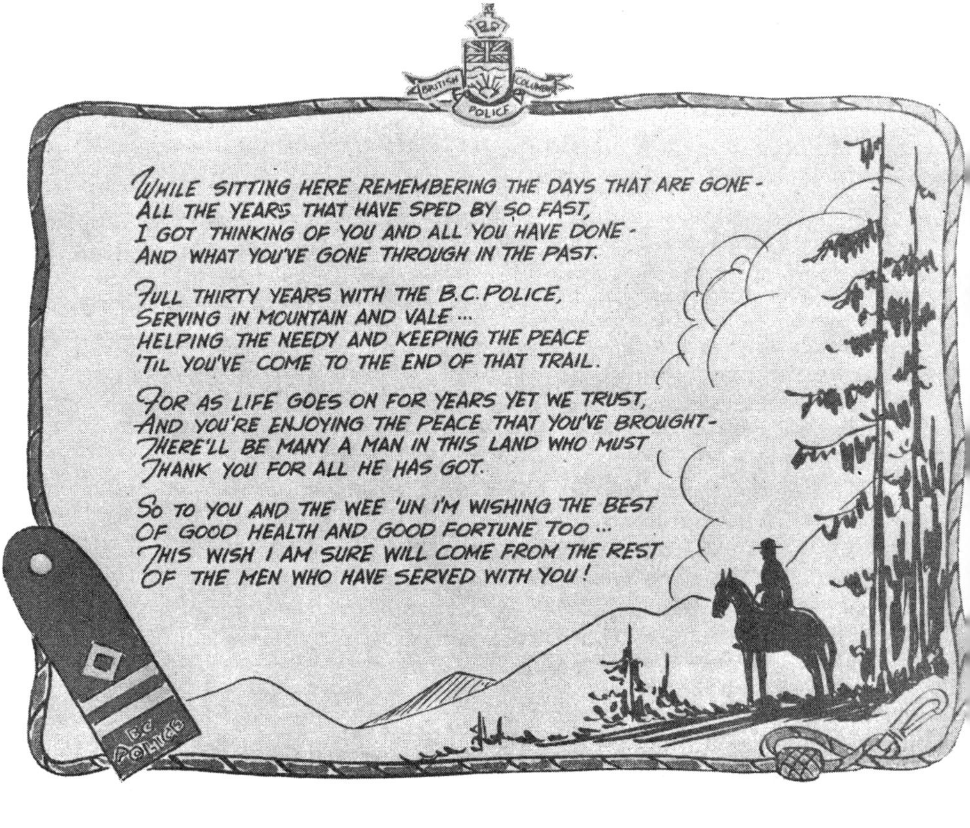
BRITISH COLUMBIA
POLICE
WHILE SITTING HERE REMEMBERING THE DAYS THAT ARE GONE -
ALL THE YEARS THAT HAVE SPED BY SO FAST,
I GOT THINKING OF YOU AND ALL YOU HAVE DONE -
AND WHAT YOU'VE GONE THROUGH IN THE PAST.
FULL THIRTY YEARS WITH THE B.C. POLICE,
SERVING IN MOUNTAIN AND VALE ...
HELPING THE NEEDY AND KEEPING THE PEACE
'TIL YOU'VE COME TO THE END OF THAT TRAIL.
FOR AS LIFE GOES ON FOR YEARS YET WE TRUST,
AND YOU'RE ENJOYING THE PEACE THAT YOU'VE BROUGHT -
THERE'LL BE MANY A MAN IN THIS LAND WHO MUST
THANK YOU FOR ALL HE HAS GOT.
SO TO YOU AND THE WEE 'UN I'M WISHING THE BEST
OF GOOD HEALTH AND GOOD FORTUNE TOO ...
THIS WISH I AM SURE WILL COME FROM THE REST
OF THE MEN WHO HAVE SERVED WITH YOU!
B.C. POLICE

The *Princess Maquinna,* one of the fleet of
freight-passenger ships which served Coastal B.C. for
over a century. On a similar vessel began the author's

NIGHTMARE ESCORT

by Corporal P. H. "Spike" Brown

Although all experiences with the B.C. Provincial Police were by no
means unpleasant, I think this story gives some idea of what things
could be like when they were. I have not used the name of the woman
in consideration of possible relatives nor identified the Detachment.
Sufficient to say that it was on the B.C. Coast in the 1930s.

We had been summoned by the superintendent of a logging company to take in charge an elderly man. Amazingly, he had made his
way alone several hundred miles from Vancouver in a Peterborough
canoe powered with a small outboard motor. He had a fixation that
there were 50 murdered RCMP officers buried in the vicinity of the
logging operations, and that the Federal Government was willing to
pay $50 for every body he located. In every other respect he was
entirely rational. We housed him in the Detachment's unoccupied
lockup as there was no other place to hold him. During the period
before he was committed to Essondale asylum near New Westminster
he proved to be a gentle and good-natured man. He and I became on

good terms, and when I was detailed to escort him down-coast I anticipated that, in spite of the objective, our trip would be an agreeable one.

The day we were departing by steamer for the overnight journey to Vancouver he and I were standing on deck. At the last minute before the gangway was removed a man hurried up it with a woman who was obviously resisting his efforts to get her on board, and disappeared with her into the ship's interior. I hardly had time to wonder about the aspects of their boarding before the man was at my side. In almost one breath he blurted that he was a doctor, the woman a violent mental case, and since I was on my way to Essondale with one charge, I might as well take two. Throwing a passage ticket and commitment papers at me (in fact, they fell on the deck), he leaped on to the ready-to-be-removed gangway and bounded down to the wharf. Here he paused momentarily to call, "Look out for yourself. She's in the last stages of a social disease!"

It all happened so quickly that I was still uttering protests that no matron had been provided and that I didn't wish the responsibility of caring for two patients when the ship backed out of the dock. With my male patient meekly trailing, I went in search of the unexpected addition to my escort to find she had been locked in a cabin. A stewardess informed me that she had been well tipped by the doctor to cater to the needs of the woman who, she said, was heavily sedated. In a sense the stewardess was acting as a matron, although not in accordance with regulations covering the transporting of a female patient. But it was the best arrangement to be expected under the peculiar circumstances. However, this did not remove the necessity of having a matron's presence after our arrival at Vancouver. I knew that I would be met with transportation as our office had been notified to expect me, but I had no way of knowing if they could have been advised of a woman being added to my escort. Locating the purser, I dictated a message he promised to dispatch to our Vancouver office by wireless.

The voyage was without incident on the way to Vancouver, the "RCMP-hunter" sharing a stateroom with me, but when we docked trouble began. I had purposely waited until all passengers had disembarked as I did not know what to expect from the distaff member of my escort with whom I had not as yet been in contact. As she was refractory boarding the ship, I thought she might be on leaving. She was! I had not known that when she was hustled to her cabin, from which she now refused to emerge, that all she had worn other than her shoes was a coat. Now she would not don the garment — worse, the sedative had worn off. Completely nude, she fiercely fought attempts of two stewardesses and the purser, and the three of them plus me when I was asked to help, to get her into the one article of her attire and out on deck. Eventually, the four of us managed to get her covered and as far as the gangway. But there, with the superhuman strength mad persons generate, she twisted away from us, threw off the coat, and ran bare and shrieking to the stern.

I was forced to pursue her alone as the ship's personnel who had assisted made themselves scarce immediately she broke loose. It was bad enough having to wrestle with a naked woman in full view of workmen on the dock. But having her scream to them that she was being kidnapped, raped, and was in dire need of rescue made my predicament much worse. The only happy factor of the moment was that my male patient, who was making clucking sounds in awe of what was going on, gave me no trouble. Rather, he was most helpful, following us about with the discarded coat. Finally, I got her covered and down the gangway.

To meet me was a Constable in uniform driving a decidedly decrepit Model A Ford sedan. It proved that he had to manipulate high gear by holding the shift in place with one hand while he steered with the other. There was no matron with him, and he knew of no message from me requesting one. To get to a telephone in order to make arrangements for a matron was out of the question. The demented woman took our full attention to keep her under any semblance of control. Several times she broke away from us and tried to hurl herself into the waters of the harbour. So, there being no chance to worry further about rules and regulations, our party got under way. Although we had considerable difficulty in getting her into the car, it was nothing to what our lady gave us when we reached Hastings Street. There she went absolutely berserk, throwing off her coat and wrapping her bare legs around the Constable's neck, causing him to narrowly miss colliding with a streetcar as he tried to steer, hold the gear in place, and see where he was going, half strangled by the legs cinched around his head. Meanwhile, the docile male patient cowered in the front seat, muttering from time to time, "Boy, is she crazy!"

I remember vividly the astounded stares of pedestrians as we passed the Pantages Theatre as they saw and heard our unclothed passenger beating on the window glass with her fists. She was loudly proclaiming, as she had shrilled on the ship, that she was being abducted and subjected to sexual indecencies. There was no use in trying to keep her in the coat. It was soon apparent that the only way to prevent us ending up as victims of a traffic accident was for me to sit on the naked woman, holding her with a head lock. Even so, she writhed loose and lashed about, kicking at the Constable's head and biting and clawing him and me. Our journey was precarious, to say the least.

All the way east on Hastings we steered an erratic course, dodging B.C. Electric interurban trams and streetcars, trucks and other vehicles. When we reached Kingsway our careening through traffic was the same. So it continued on that route through Burnaby, into and through New Westminster, and on to Essondale. Every foot we battled that thrashing, screaming, clawing, and biting woman, trying to avoid the rakings of her finger nails and the sharpness of her teeth, perspiration streaming down our faces. It was a hellish, real-life nightmare I trust I will never have to know again.

We thought that when we reached our destination we would be

sure of help. There would be those expert in handling such a person as we had struggled with for almost two hours in that slow-moving car. We pulled up to the entrance of Essondale exhausted. Leaving the Constable and my male patient who had valiantly tried to assist us to cope with the woman the best they could, I sprinted into the building. There was no one in sight except a nurse seated at a reception table. Panting, I quickly explained our situation, asking that she have an adequate number of the hospital's staff take over and suggesting that some means of restraint be provided. I can recall exactly what she said as she sat with a pen poised over some papers.

"Come now, Constable Brown, relax! You're making a mountain out of a molehill. First thing we have to do is look over the commitment papers so I can make out admitting forms." She held out her hand expecting me to give her the documents, and added, "Please take a chair while you wait."

I know I shouted at her, "Wait? The woman's stark naked and we can't do a thing with her! She's been fighting us like a wildcat all the way from Vancouver! For God's sake, do something!"

She raised a supercilious eyebrow. "All in good time," she smirked. "We have procedures to follow!"

At that moment the doors to the office burst open and in ran our nude charge with the Constable at her heels. At a lesser pace behind was my male patient. The bare-as-she-was-born woman was behind the nurse and into a nearby record room before she could have been prevented. In any event, in my exasperation I made no attempt to stop her. She began ripping pages from ledgers and emptying cases of filed cards on the floor. I don't think I've ever seen a change of attitude develop in anyone as suddenly as it did in that nurse. She jumped from her chair, crossed a hall as though propelled by a spring, and began pushing what were evidently alarm buttons. The door of an elevator opened. As if they had been waiting in it, out came two husky nurses and two orderlies at the double. The naked rampaging woman was covered with a blanket, strapped to a stretcher and whisked into the elevator in what seemed a split second. Nor was there any thought of forms being written up. That was the last we saw of her. Sadly, but perhaps a blessing, she died three days later.

A doctor arrived and insisted that the Constable, my male patient and I wash thoroughly with an antiseptic solution he provided in consideration of the physical condition of the woman with whom we had been in contact. Then I went through the necessary formalities of admitting both patients, but not dealing with the nurse I had at first encountered. For some reason she had disappeared.

I shook hands with the RCMP-hunter as I left. "Boy!" he grinned, "and they say I'm nuts!"

A Detachment Office with no phone, swearing a court
oath on the dictionary, and an escaped prisoner who
mailed his handcuffs back. It was all part of

POLICING LILLOOET IN 1914

by 1st Class Constable Gilbert F. "Gil" Killam

In the summer of 1914 I was transferred from Barkerville to Lillooet
which was a very busy place because of construction of the Pacific
Great Eastern Railway. There were grading and rail-laying gangs (pick
and shovel), as well as a large bridge construction crew erecting a
sizeable trestle high over the Fraser River on the outskirts of town.
Three saloons were in operation, and with a numerous Indian population in 27 settlements I felt I earned my $85 a month.

There was a small room off the police office which I turned into
sleeping quarters, saving me $10 a month, the cost of a room at the
hotel where I took my meals. If I needed conveyance beyond the town
a saddle horse was available for $1 a day. When need be, as when
bringing in prisoners, I hired an automobile.

In the lockup were six wooden cells — four for men and two for
women, with a partition and a stout door between. The lockup was
seldom empty, and to police the town and surrounding territory day
and night while by necessity being jailer as well, kept me busy.
Prisoners were fed food I was required to carry to them from a Chinese
restaurant. Allowance by the Attorney-General's Department was 15
cents per meal. No one but the Chinaman at that cafe would supply
meals at that price. I laid in some rolled oats so the drunks could feed
themselves by making porridge on the stove in the lockup, thus cutting

In 1913 the author was sent to Barkerville, his equipment "a
badge, gun, handcuffs and baton." The next year he was
transferred to Lillooet.At the time stagecoaches which had
served the Cariboo for over 50 years were being replaced
by autos.The one at top, opposite page, at Clinton on the
Cariboo Wagon Road in 1907 was the first to
travel the historic route.

Away from the main road, however, horses remained the
main means of transportation, typified by the opposite
photo of Lillooet's main street in the early 1900s. Reflecting
the community's gold-rush heritage, the street was wide
enough for a bull team of eight or more oxen
and a wagon to be turned around.

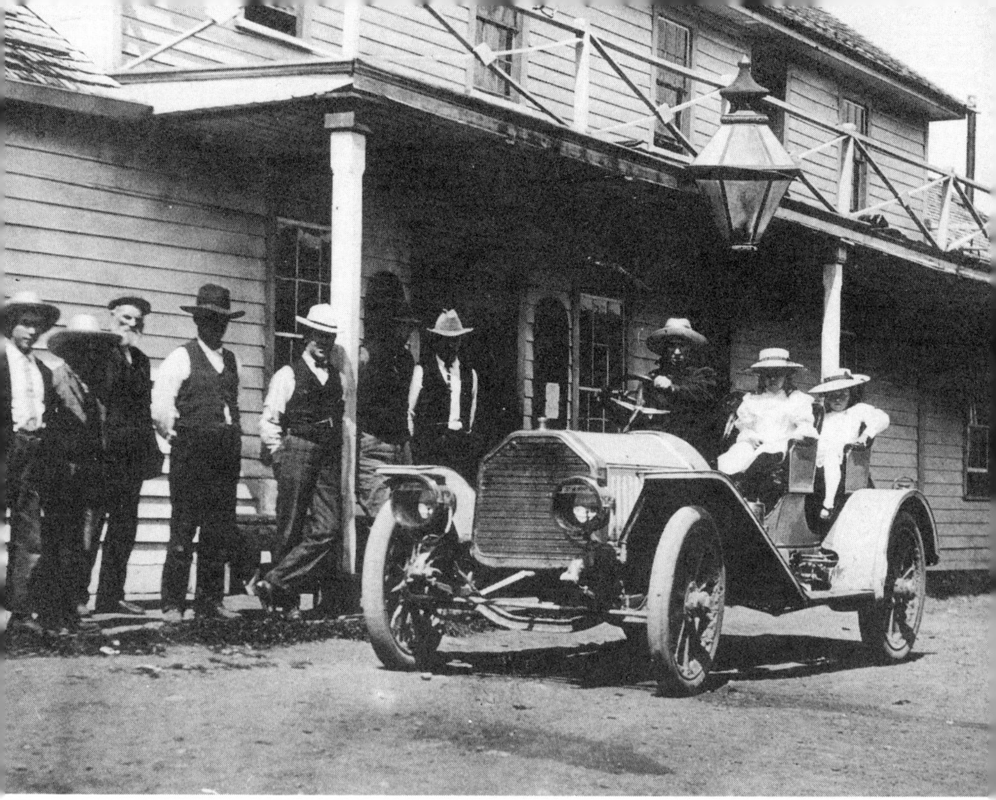

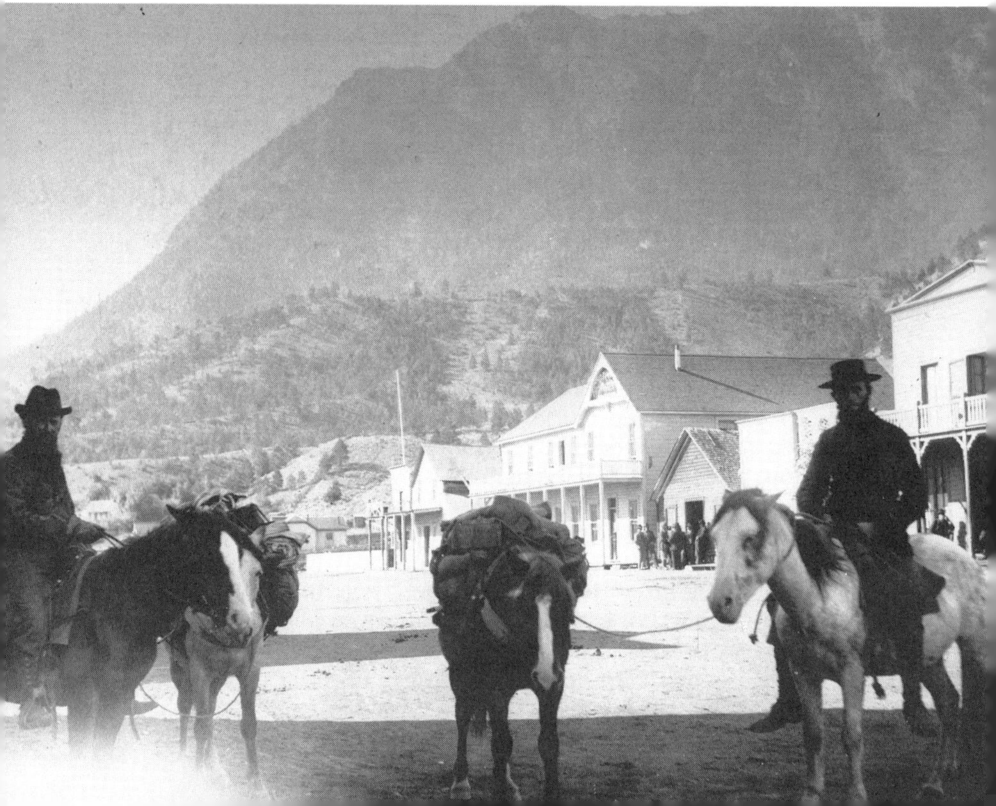

down on the 15 cents allowance so I could supply more substantial meals to other prisoners.

When prisoners had to be escorted to Kamloops jail or Oakalla, I would leave the most reliable man I could find as a Special in charge of the Detachment. Then I took off for Lytton, 45 miles away, with maybe two owner-driven autos. These were touring cars which proceeded at 20 m.p.h. I would have the top down on the second car and would sit on the back rest of the rear seat of the car in front so I could keep my eye on all my charges, maybe with my revolver in hand if a limited supply of handcuffs indicated that precaution.

I only experienced one attempt at escape, and a futile one at that. On arrival at Lytton where Constable Bill Steward was then stationed, the prisoners would be locked in that Detachment's cells to await trains to convey them to their destinations — Kamloops, if they were sentenced to serve time there, or to Oakalla as need be. I made the trips with them and returned to Lytton with all dispatch possible. Up to 40 convictions a month was not unusual. In those days escorts from "Up Country" did not go into Vancouver. We detrained at Westminster Junction, took the C.P.R. branch into New Westminster, then went by the B.C. Electric Railway's tram to Royal Oak Station, and walked our prisoners through bush, down Royal Oak Avenue to Oakalla!

Heating of the Lillooet lockup was by wood stoves, and a good supply of hardwood cordwood had to be ready in the fall against the winter cold. Sawing it was no problem. There were always local bar-flies serving short sentences and the exercise they got when in confinement was good for their physiques. Their chums on the loose would usually cache a bottle of "saw lubricant" in the woodpile which made the labour more congenial. They all knew I knew it was there. To prevent it being confiscated depended on them, so the sawing usually went smoothly. It was a matter of reciprocity. Those who did the sawing were aware that it would be their turn to supply the "lubricant" when their pals' turn came to work on the woodpile. It was safe to leave those occupied with sawing as there was no place for them to go, and to some the lockup was better in many ways than what they called home.

Supplying liquor to Indians was a common occurrence. Trouble with the men working on the railway and Indian women was frequent, too. On a hill back of town five prostitutes from the Coast occupied two houses. The attitude of the citizens (from which I took my cue) was that they were tolerable, and during railway construction an advisable requisite. I let them know their presence depended on their good behavior and if they caused trouble they would be down the road in short order. They succeeded in their own policing.

During that time the District Headquarters was at Clinton, with Chief Constable Frank Aitken in charge. The District also had a Senior Constable in its personnel who, in my time, was Bill Spiller (in later years an Inspector commanding a Division). As we were in pre-uniform times, Constables from one territory might come into another without being recognized. On one occasion Bill Spiller was in Lillooet during his travels and came upon an Indian woman and a railroad worker busily engaged with each other and a bottle in the bush. He brought them into the lockup, and they were later taken to court. Court lighting (also in the jail) consisted of kerosene hand lamps. As a consequence, court procedures were often conducted in what amounted to gloom. When the Bible happened to be in the neighboring Government Agent's office with which it was shared, and the court was called to session, frequently a closed dictionary of similar size and appearance would be used as a substitute, being careful to keep its title toward the floor. No one was ever the wiser!

The magistrate was a doughty old gentleman of 80 who had been in the Cariboo since his youth and thoroughly knew the customs and habits of the inhabitants. He was a bachelor, his attire when conducting court was shirt sleeves, the shirt open at the neck, over which he wore an ancient suit vest exhibiting the residues of the menus at the hotel where he took his meals. As his eyesight curtailed his efforts he didn't bother shaving.

When Bill Spiller's prisoners were arraigned before him the man appeared first, charged with supplying liquor to an Indian. He was fined $500 or six months in jail. In the case of the Indian woman — whom I will call Matilda Johnnie — Bill had laid a charge of vagrancy which under the existing statutes covered a multitude of sins. Matilda was plainly not a person of bright intellect so the magistrate suggested a plea of not guilty on her behalf and called on Bill to state his case. He then asked Matilda what she had to say. "Yah," was her reply.

His Honor found her guilty, adding a mild reprove. Then, turning to Bill he asked, "Mr. Spiller, I presume you agree that as well as this being a court of law it is also a court of justice?"

Puzzled by the unexpected question, Bill replied, "Yes, I guess so."

"Good," said the beak. Then, turning to the defendant, he ordered: "Matilda Johnnie, stand up."

She stood. He contemplated her in silence. Then, speaking slowly and tapping his finger to emphasize his words, he gave his decision.

"If those women on the hill can practice their calling undisturbed," he said, moving his arm in the general direction of the brothels, "Matilda Johnnie can practice her calling in the bush undisturbed. Case dismissed."

Bill stared at him in silence. His jaw dropped, then he threw back his head and burst into laughter.

My next experience could well have had serious consequences — for me, at any rate. Before leaving Barkerville my friends there had said: "Going to Lillooet eh? Wait until you come up against Big Tom. He'll be a handful!"

Each fall a caravan of Indians (none living nearer than Quesnel) drove from the Lower Cariboo to Barkerville to harvest huckleberries growing in profusion in that area. It seems that one year Big Tom, who hailed from Lillooet, was among them. He was a very able man, I was told, but liked alcohol. He had run foul of the law, had been arrested, then bested the Constable and three other men who had come to his aid. Then he had melted into the scenery with handcuffs on one wrist. Later he had thoughtfully mailed them to the Constable.

My adventure with Big Tom occurred on an Indian Reserve some three miles from Lillooet south of Cayuse Creek. In Lillooet was a Dominion Government Telegraph Office which had the only telephone available to the public — I didn't even have one at the Detachment. In charge was a wiry little man of probably 115 pounds who one evening came looking for me. A merchant who had a general store and a phone about a mile from Lillooet had rung him in an excited and incoherent manner and asked that I be notified that I was needed urgently.

At that time I had a fairly reliable Special Constable and I commandeered one of the Model T taxis in town. I was about to be on my way when the telegrapher said that as he had closed his office for the night he would like to come along. I was dubious, but as he pleaded to accompany us, I agreed. We drove to the store and were informed by a half-breed rancher that while he was en-route to his farm farther down the Fraser he had been dispossessed of his team by a drunken Indian.

Accompanying the rancher, we crossed a bridge over the creek to the Indian settlement and were guided to a cabin where the troublesome Indian was alleged to be. The half-breed then faded, perhaps discreetly, into the night. I unceremoniously opened the door of the cabin and entered. The one room had a couple of homemade bunks and chairs at one end, and a stove, table, etc., at the other. A group of Indians were at the bed end, and on one of the bunks sat one of them with two whisky bottles standing on the floor before him.

I started in his direction. As I did he rose to his feet, grasped a bottle by its neck and came at me. I leaped forward, swung a punch and knocked the bottle from his hand as it was about to descend on my head. Quickly seizing his wrist with my right hand I yanked his body across my hip and used his momentum to effect a throw. He went through the air to land on his belly.

The cabin was of flimsy construction and when his bulk hit the floor everything shook like an aspen. He was a man of over 200 lbs, and since I was then 160, the exertion of throwing him put me off balance. But as he hit the floor the little telegrapher was on his back like a terrier with a hammerlock.

I staggered across the room to fall on the big Indian, too, and got a grip on his free wrist. I was carrying a pair of the old Bean handcuffs, and snapped a ring of them around his wrist. But to my horror, they wouldn't meet to lock.

Hearing the command "Stand back all of you!" I glanced upward. The Special was standing over us with drawn gun and keeping the other Indians at bay. The jitney driver was in the entrance to the cabin. Fluent in the Indian tongue, he was advising them to keep out of the fracas. I wasn't sorry! The telegrapher held his hammerlock while I struggled with my hold and called to the Special to give me his handcuffs which were Towers, then in more general use than mine. I

As Constable Killam quickly discovered, officers were responsible for looking after their prisoners. To provide accommodation for policemen and prisoners, upwards of 100 lockups were built throughout the province. They generally consisted of one room with cells. Each was sparsely furnished with a stove, table, chairs and a bed, although on Mayne Island in 1897 the officer had to provide his own bed. The one above is at Atlin in 1899. From left is Constable Harry Heal; Mrs. J. Clay, a well-known mining woman; and Constable E. A. Desbaisy.

In addition to being very basically furnished, they were not much bigger than a modern living room. The one on Mayne Island, for instance, was 15 by 23 feet. They were also economical to build, the Mayne lockup costing $320. Thanks to the work of the Mayne Island Horticultural Society, it has been preserved.

The Soda Creek lockup in the Cariboo also still survives, although abandoned. Built in the early 1890s, it is in remarkably good condition, below, and should also be preserved as a Heritage Building. The back cover shows it about 1902 with Constable Robert Pyper and his horse, Duke.

found they met around the wrists of the thrashing Indian — but in their last notch. Then, with his hands secured behind him, we got him into the car and headed for Lillooet.

After our prisoner was safely locked in a cell without further resistance, the jitney driver who was still with us remarked, "You were lucky to get Big Tom. They usually can't bring him in."

I turned and looked at him. "Is that...?" I started to say, then paused and drew a deep breath. He merely grinned.

That was our first — and what proved to be our only — encounter with Big Tom, for which I was thankful, wondering what might be the outcome if we tangled again. I had no regret now in having permitted the telegrapher to accompany me since the success of the evening was as much to his credit as to mine.

The following morning when Big Tom was sober it would be difficult to find a more genial or kindly man, which I learned was his usual nature.

With the Lillooet tribe of Indians the head chief was James Retasket, known as Tyee Jimmy. He was very gentlemanly. I never saw him but he was dressed in a neat and immaculate blue suit, white shirt, black bow tie, and bowler hat. He was not of large stature, but stately in person and manner. He was intelligent and fair in all his dealings, much respected and of great influence throughout the tribe. He was held in high regard also by government departments and their personnel.

The Indian community had its own Indian police appointed by the tribal council which looked after matters strictly within Indian jurisdiction. I could depend on them, particularly one Tesant Bones with whom I became friendly. He often acted as intermediary and translator.

Lillooet was then a typical frontier town with tin-horn gambling and every other aspect except gunplay — that is, in the general sense. Shooting affairs, however, were part of the country and of the times. Not long after my arrival I experienced my first. The outcome was in one way humorous, although it could have resulted in a murder charge.

I received a message that there had been a shooting some 20 miles to the east. A man had been wounded, but there were no fatalities. As the railway builders had established a small hospital with a doctor and a nurse not far from the jail, I got a good auto stage, picked up the doctor and away we went.

It turned out that an Italian farm laborer and an Indian girl had been living together without benefit of clergy. But being an amorously ambitious man he had not been satisfied with things as they were and developed an eye for his common-law wife's sister. She was receptive to his admiration and they met clandestinely in the evenings, the bush being plentiful. The No. 1 lady in the triangle got suspicious. Silently, as is the way of Indians, she took steps to exercise her disapproval. She became a sleuth, watching where her man went, and witnessed subsequent proceedings. He usually rode to his tryst on horseback, keeping the animal near while he and his love melted into each others' arms.

It came to pass that No. 1 gal was waiting for them one night with a .30-30 Winchester. Observing her, the man sprang for his horse, but he wasn't quick enough. A bullet got him, not where she intended, but fortunately not puncturing a vital spot.

When the doctor and I arrived he was lying on his saddle blanket face down, having been assisted to that position by Indians who had been attracted by the gunfire. As he leaped onto his horse the bullet had got him sideways, missing bones. But what that soft-nosed slug at point-blank range had done in a full sweep across his posterior you wouldn't believe! A good part of it was shot away. It would be a long time before he sat down again!

Learning what was necessary from the wounded man, I left him in the care of the doctor and went to apprehend the Indian Annie Oakley. Her home was a third of a mile distant. On my way to it I reflected that the .38 Colt revolver I was carrying would be little consolation against a .30-30 rifle. In addition, the woman would have house windows to shoot through while I had to approach her over open ground.

I had the driver of the car come within sight of the house. I left my gun with him and went on foot the remainder of the way, entering the yard with palms stretched out to indicate I was unarmed, hoping the Lord was on my side. Then I saw something beyond all I had expected. Looking back at the car I could hardly believe my eyes. The woman was sitting in the front seat beside the driver. Unconcernedly, she was waiting to be transported to jail.

We then made a rough litter of boughs and placed it across the tonneau of the car on which we laid the wounded man, while the doctor and I occupied the back seat so we could watch his condition. It was a rough 20-mile ride but he made it. His paramour didn't turn her head once to look at him.

At the Fall Assizes she was sentenced to a short prison term although few persons connected with the trial felt she should be punished. But as she had plead guilty with stoic Indian indifference, feeling satisfaction in what she had accomplished in chastising her wayward Romeo, there was no choice but to convict her.

By now World War One had started and my thoughts, like those of many others, strayed in that direction. I wanted to enlist and applied for leave, but Chief Aitken told me I could be as useful in B.C. as elsewhere. Nevertheless, being determined, before spring had passed I was in the army at the Coast. While in Lillooet I had realized that while a Constable had considerable influence within his territory and was part and parcel of the community, it was up to him to use his standing judiciously.

PRINCE RUPERT'S TRAGIC FOURTH OF JULY

The U.S. sailors ashore in Prince Rupert lamented the lack of fireworks to celebrate the Fourth of July. A taxi driver provided a grim substitute.

by Deputy Commissioner Cecil Clark

There is a jesting remark applied to rather wettish Prince Rupert that when it stops raining, people are out of sorts. July 4, 1938, fell in the middle of a dry spell and one of that city's residents, 24-year-old Mike Gurvich, was definitely in a bad mood. The result of his ill humor was the town topic before nightfall.

On that particular day a United States destroyer, the *Hopkins*, was in port on a visit. Sailors crowded the sidewalks looking for diversion and were disappointed that the Glorious Fourth was not celebrated in

Officer G. H. Clark,
a decorated World War One veteran,
whose bullet killed the gunman.

The Royal Hotel where Gurvich was killed.

Murdered Inspector Service
left a wife and five children.

Prince Rupert's courthouse (in the
crescent) where Gurvich murdered
the two officers, and the dock area
where he violated parking regulations.

Canada. They missed the fireworks, the bands and parades, but especially the fireworks. Around two that afternoon the beer parlor of Jim Zarelli's Royal Hotel was packed with American seamen who were sure of one thing — if there were no fireworks, then the Canadian beer had an authority that lent color to the occasion. Little did they suspect that there was to be a grim substitute for the excitement they missed.

Mike Gurvich and his two older brothers operated a taxi service, and he would not conform with a bylaw governing the parking of public conveyances at the Canadian National's dock. After being warned repeatedly about his negligence, he was served with a summons by Corporal George H. Clark of the B.C. Provincial Police, responsible for enforcing the law not only in Prince Rupert from its City Detachment, but also the territory extending from Alaska south to Ocean Falls, and from the Queen Charlotte Islands to Terrace. This massive area was administered by 45-year-old Inspector William "Big Bill" Service from D Division headquarters located in the courthouse.

Gurvich was furious about receiving the summons, and embarked on a course which was to end in tragedy. Perhaps his reaction stemmed from paranoia lingering from five years before when he had been a patient in Essondale Mental Hospital. Perhaps it was to some degree fostered by the hot blood of his Albanian ancestry. Whatever the cause of his unfounded ire, he consulted a lawyer, contending that he had been improperly served with the summons as it had been left at his office. Although his lawyer advised him to accept it, Gurvich was not satisfied. He confronted Corporal Clark on the street and strongly voiced his objection. He was told by the officer he would be required, regardless of his opinions, to appear in court. Gurvich then drove away. Shortly afterward Corporal Harold Raybone, skipper of one of the force's coastal patrol boats, was walking on McBride Avenue to the courthouse and stopped to chat with a logger acquaintance. He noticed Gurvich drive by in his taxi in the same direction in which he was headed, then soon return at a fast speed.

At his office in the courthouse, which was apart from the room used by Inspector Service and other D Division personnel, Corporal D. W. Taylor thought he heard a series of muffled explosions somewhere along the basement corridor. He left his typewriter and looked up and down the passage, but saw nothing except a man disappearing upstairs at the end of the hall.

What he had heard, he thought, could have been backfires of some vehicle in the street, but as there was an eerie silence in the building and he was still puzzled, he checked the Divisional Office.

There, he was shocked to see 50-year-old Sergeant Bob Gibson lying on the floor in a welter of blood, a bullet hole in the back of his head. Racing around a counter he found Inspector Service, also shot in the head. Chairs were overturned, and from the position of one he decided Gibson had been sitting typing, his back to the door, when he was cut down. It seemed he had heard four explosions in pairs. Glancing quickly about he noticed a bullet hole in the floor, and another high in a wall.

He thought of the phone, but couldn't find it. Not knowing it was beneath a desk where it had fallen when Service collapsed, he dashed to his own office to call the City Detachment for assistance. As he left his office he met Corporal Raybone and hurriedly told him what had happened.

Department of Mines Inspector Jack Graham and his stenographer, Helen Walker, came from their offices upstairs. They had heard the shots and were sure that the only person they had seen leaving the building after the blasts was Mike Gurvich. Taylor now realized he must have been the man he had seen vanishing around a corner of the passage and very likely responsible for the shootings.

Inspecting the prone figures, Raybone exclaimed, "Gibson's still alive! Call a doctor and an ambulance."

In response to Taylor's telephoned report, Corporal George Clark, who had served the summons to Gurvich, arrived accompanied by Constable Terry Stewart. There was a hurried consultation. Raybone, remembering he had seen Mike Gurvich driving toward the courthouse and returning from its area, remarked, "If it was Gurvich, we'd better find him, and quick!"

Leaving Taylor to await the doctor and ambulance, Clark, Raybone, and Stewart headed in a police car for the suspected man's taxi stand near the Royal Hotel.

Before their arrival, Rosario Mazzel, a cab driver, had been surprised to see Gurvich pull up opposite the hotel and get out of his car with a revolver in his hand. "I got 'em!" was Mike's triumphant shout to the wondering Mazzel.

"Got who?"

"Service and Gibson. I got 'em both!" cried Mike and disappeared, still with gun in hand, into the hotel's beer parlor.

"Gimme a beer," he snapped breathlessly to waiter Eddie Smith. The startled Smith, eyeing the weapon in Gurvich's hand, hastened to comply. Mike gulped the beer, and stood on tiptoe to look above the muslin curtain that screened the lower half of the window, peering into the street. Wild-eyed and muttering incoherent threats, he yelled at Smith, "Gimme another beer!"

By now the sailors crowding the premises were taking an interest in the strange and excited customer. Suddenly Gurvich slammed down his glass and headed for the side door of the parlor. As he made his way to the street, the police trio swung around a corner and braked to a slamming stop.

As they piled out of the car, Gurvich faced them, gun at the ready.

Terry Stewart, in plainclothes and unarmed since it was his day off, did the logical thing — he used the police car as a shield.

Raybone and Clark, guns drawn, advanced on Gurvich. He backed toward the hotel. Clark shouted at him to drop his gun. The answer was a shot.

Raybone and Clark fired, and Gurvich shot again.

George Clark said later that he thought if Gurvich had used four bullets at the courthouse, and a fifth on the street when he was first encountered, his gun might have been emptied. But the wanted man had reloaded.

Backing from the advancing police, Gurvich gained the shelter of the beer parlor.

"Keep him busy there," said Raybone to Clark. "I'll slip around to the side door and block him." Before he could make that move both officers saw Gurvich peering at them from above the curtain of the parlor's window.

Both fired in split-second reaction. One of their bullets caught their quarry between his eyes. When he fell it was among the sailors from the U.S.S. *Hopkins* who had mourned that Prince Rupert had no fireworks on the Fourth of July.

Sergeant Gibson died a few hours later, never regaining consciousness. Inspector Service had died instantly. His passing left five small daughters fatherless.

At the coroner's inquest a few days later, ballistic evidence linked Gurvich's gun with the double killing at the courthouse. The jury praised the swift and courageous action of the police. That it was swift is indicated by the fact that Dr. Hankison, who answered Taylor's call, drove by the police exchanging shots with the murderer outside the hotel.

From Headquarters at Victoria a month later came promotions for Clark, Raybone and Stewart. Harold Raybone served in the RCAF during World War Two, but did not return to police service. Instead, for a change of pace, he became skipper of a whaler. Later, he was in command of one of the Navy's auxiliary vessels at Esquimalt.

During the war, Clark, who had won the Military Cross in World War One, rose in rank until absorbed by the RCMP as Inspector in 1950 when that force took over policing B.C. Pensioned soon afterwards, he became a well-known police magistrate at Edmonton.

Terry Stewart was absorbed by the RCMP and rose in rank.

No doubt Gurvich had a homicidal antipathy to police, and perhaps felt he would signal his resentment by killing Service as head of all police in Prince Rupert. Gibson, who happened to be in the same room, was an innocent victim of the crazed man. Whatever the reason, it was a cold-blooded affair for neither of the slain men were armed. Service was in plainclothes, and Gibson's Sam Browne belt with holstered gun hung on a peg. Both must have been taken completely by surprise. Service, whose name was synonymous with bravery, would never have been shot without a struggle, even though unarmed.

Ford's cabin, over 100 roadless miles from the nearest store. The old trapper came out once a year, backpacking everything through the miles of wilderness.

MISSING

The old trapper bragged that he lived "tougher" than any Indian. The author agreed after travelling 415 wilderness miles — over 200 on foot — to search for him.

by Constable H. O. Jamieson

Hugh Ford, a taciturn prospector and trapper, lived alone on the upper reaches of the Stikine River. Once a year he made his trip to Dease Lake or Telegraph Creek, bringing a few skins to be traded for flour, beans, tea and sugar. It was Ford's boast that he lived "tougher" than any Indian. The Indians did not deny this statement. In fact, few of them ever travelled through Ford's harsh country.

Towards the end of September he had not made his annual trip out for supplies and it became clear that some calamity had befallen the old man. Since part of my duties was searching for missing people, I drove to Dease Lake to make arrangements with Jimmy McGregor, a young and husky Scotsman, to accompany me into the Upper Stikine Country. Jimmy claimed to know part of this country, having been through one winter with his dog team. It was, however, still too early in the season to use a sleigh. We decided we would take two of his dogs and three of mine as packers, whilst we would carry our own sleeping robes and spare clothing on packboards. I have hated packboards ever since.

Returning to Telegraph Creek, I spent the next few days getting ready for the long journey. Dog-packs had to be overhauled, supplies purchased, and, considering the relatively unexplored country through which we were to travel, our proposed routes carefully check-ed on the maps available.

I had a prisoner in jail at Telegraph Creek, an Indian named Mike McKluskey. Mike was delighted when I told him he was to come with us as a general handyman. He hated to chop wood and do the other chores around the jail. As a result he required no urging to roll his ragged bed-roll in order to spend the balance of his visit with the Law under the stars in his beloved Cassiar.

Unable to borrow a light enough sleeping robe to backpack, I was obliged to take my cheap snug robe. Never exactly snug, on this trip it cost me many hours of sleeplessness and misery.

On the morning of September 30, 1945, I bundled Mike and my three dogs — Major, Colonel and Marten — in the back of a pick-up truck. I kissed my wife goodbye and with excited dogs and a cheerful Indian we headed out into the unknown.

The sky was lowering as we started. I fervently hoped we would get to Dease Lake before the grey clouds began to discharge their rain. The road was that in name only. In the virtually unsettled area it could take truckers days to cover the 73 miles, and it wasn't unusual to spend several of them in one mudhole.

The weeping curtain of clouds came closer, and just as we began to descend the dreaded Tuya River hill, the rain came pelting down. In a few moments the little truck began to slide ominously, causing me to perspire gently and causing Mike's dark eyes to roll in apprehension. However, we made the bottom of the hill. Mike and I put on chains and off we went, ploughing through mud and water up hill and down dale, until at 64 Mile Bob Farrell and his old truck, christened Clarabelle, showed up through the mist. Poor Bob was in trouble. He was on his way from Telegraph Creek to Dease Lake with a big load of groceries when Clarabelle threw a piston out of the side of the engine block. A spare engine and help was required. Therefore, I loaned Bob my tent to give him shelter for the night, while we went back for a spare engine and help. The delay was annoying, but it was all part of the job.

Arriving back at Dease Lake after this little interlude, I found Jimmy and Mike had all the packs made up and were set to go. The dogs seemed excited at the prospect of action. After a lunch in Jimmy's trapping cabin, I bade my truck a reluctant goodbye and off we went.

From the beginning it was interesting to note the behavior of the dogs. My three dogs frisked about in the bush in high good humor, but Jimmy's more seasoned pack-dogs attended strictly to business. They kept up the steady, characteristic half-trot, taking no part in the playful antics of Major, Colonel or Marten. By the time we turned off the main Boulder Creek Trail and swung down the Tanzilla River, the differences between the seasoned veterans and the enthusiastic amateurs were apparent. Major was doing fairly well but we repeatedly had to wait for Marten and Colonel. In fact, when we arrived at Jimmy's trapping cabin, where we stayed the night, Colonel did not struggle in for a full hour and was obviously exhausted. So much for the first day on the trail.

The following day, October 2, was dull and grey. A fine rain was falling as we set off at dawn. To make things easier for Colonel, we had saddled him with only a 15-pound pack. But after the first half mile he set up such a pitiful howling that we were forced to take off his pack and distribute it among the other dogs and ourselves. This did not make either of us feel any better. We were already carrying our sleeping robes, spare clothing and rifles. So it was a tired and sullen party that slipped and floundered over muskeg and through dripping trees to arrive at Jimmy McGregor's second and last trapping cabin.

At dawn the following morning it was much colder and the weather had cleared. We continued up the Tanzilla past Gnat Creek and decided to cross the summit higher up rather than follow Gnat, which Jimmy reported to be full of underbrush and deadfalls.

Near the head of the river, at the foot of the pass, we were forced to stop and make a temporary camp as Marten and Colonel were so far behind. I had to send Mike back to bring them in.

Jimmy's dogs were standing up well under their 35-pound packs, so, after a cup of hot tea and a biscuit, we decided to leave my three sissies here in charge of Mike. His instructions, which he did not much relish, were to wait five days. If we did not show up at the end of that period, he was to take the dogs and return to Dease Lake. It promised to be a lonely vigil, and it was a crestfallen Indian with whom we left all the supplies we could not use. Then Jimmy, I and the dogs headed for the pass.

This was rather a serious business. Our quest for Hugh Ford was taking us into unknown country with skeleton rations. Up the pass we went, scrambling over huge boulders, through buck-brush as tall as a man. At the summit there were blue lakes which we skirted. We came to vast, prairie-like openings of brush and grass through which caribou had worn foot-deep trails. In the evening we set our lean-to canvas in a deep ravine on the Ptarmigan Creek side. Snow was beginning to fall. We rustled up a night's supply of wood and soon had a hearty meal of bannock and beans and tea. Then into our sleeping robes, where I was to spend the first of many shivering nights listening to Jimmy's loud and maddening snores.

The following day we continued down the pass until we arrived on the banks of Ptarmigan Creek. Here we saw the remnants of the old trail of the 1870s used to herd cattle, horses, mules, and even turkeys from the southern Cariboo to the meat hungry gold camps of the Dease River.

The balance of the morning we spent travelling down the creek, and in warm sunshine it was almost pleasant. That night, by contrast, we spent in another snow storm, drying our clothes, massaging blistered feet, and finally, through sheer exhaustion, going to sleep despite my companion's unmusical snoring. The poor dogs had no energy but to gulp their corn meal mush and curl up for the night.

Snow had changed to rain in the morning as we stiffly turned out to struggle through another day. But by the time we had fought our way through swamps, brush and gloomy ravines to the banks of the Stikine River, we were too tired to care what the weather did. This was Ford's country, almost unpenetrated by white men and shunned by Indians. Whatever possesses men to live in such isolated, total wilderness, and what tradition of service sends us on their trail? We often read of the exploits of our brother policemen, the RCMP, and their gruelling patrols in Canada's frozen Northland, and to them I take off my hat. But they are not the only ones. The B.C. Police, too, have a long standing record of justice and help for all. I thought of these things as we clambered and slid along the banks of the Stikine, sometimes forced by huge mud banks to take to the dripping and gloomy bush.

Here, in dank spruce swamps, the huge bull moose held their nuptials. Twice we were rushed furiously as the animals suspected us of being rivals for the affections of their lady-loves. Darkness found us making camp under a huge spruce in about 12 inches of sticky snow.

By noon next day we were on the bank of the McBride River. We crossed in zero weather, wading up to our hips and lining the dogs over with ropes. We did not bother to remove our water-filled shoes or sodden clothes as we were sure Ford had a cabin nearby and looked forward to a pleasant evening in a warm cabin. Sure enough, on the opposite bank we found several tree stumps and evidence of a campsite. We progressed up the river, and came upon a well cut trail. There were two unsprung traps under trees.

Then we came upon it. There, in the center of a small clearing, stood Ford's cabin. The whole place was hushed and still, even the dogs seemed aware that tragedy had visited this quiet place. Jimmy and I carefully scanned the snow for tracks or other signs of life. There were none.

Hanging above the front door were several mouse-eaten lynx, wolf and coyote skins. As I opened the door I could see only packrats had occupied this miserable hovel for a long time. Piles of dead leaves and twigs were everywhere. They rustled eerily as Jimmy and I set foot within. On the bed were blankets, thrown back by Ford as he got out of bed that fateful morning. His big alarm clock was on a bench near the bed, and on the table the remains of his breakfast — boiled wild rice and salt.

Not another edible thing was in the cabin. On the rusty stove stood a huge pot of the same stuff. Ford must have laboriously gathered the wild rice from a nearby swamp. It is hard to imagine a man living for long on such stuff, even a man who boasted he was tougher than any Indian. But there was the evidence.

Neither Jimmy nor I cared to spend the night in such a stinking hole. We continued on, following a well cut trail along the Stikine. Finally, when we were both nearly ready to drop from exhaustion, we came to a second clearing and another silent, empty cabin. This contained not a scrap of food, simply ammunition and salt.

We soon had a good fire going in the small camp stove, while by candle I examined the place for signs of recent habitation. There were none. Ford had been using bear skins for blankets, with moose and bear hocks skinned out to form rough mukluks for shoes.

Next morning, October 7, found me nursing an infected left foot which I bathed and rubbed. Jimmy went up the Kehlechoa River for some miles, but returned saying it was no use to continue the search. It was obvious that Ford was dead. After some discussion we agreed to abandon the search, leaving a note for Ford, if he did turn up.

Early next morning we were again at Ford's main camp where I took a list of what equipment he had. I made note of the fact that he had not planted his garden, which to me proved he met his death early the previous spring, probably around May. After leaving a note on the table here also, we started our long journey back to Dease Lake.

By now we were living on grouse, bannock and tea with a little sugar and grease. Up the river we went, crossing it in swift water, pushing through dismal swamps and spruce forests, where the rutting moose made the nights hideous with their bawling. Once I was forced to wound a moose in the leg with my .22 rifle before he would give us the right of way. I hated to but had no choice and certainly did not want to kill him with a larger rifle. On the evening of the third day we camped at timberline in a howling blizzard at Caribou Pass. Next day, I left Jimmy behind with the dogs and about four in the afternoon, when the pale sun was going down behind the mountains, I again rounded the bend in the road to see the welcome sight of my little truck. There, too, squatted over a smoky fire was Mike. Back in the bush, howling their heads off with joy at seeing me, were my three dogs. Mike grinned widely at my approach and said that after waiting the five days, feeding the dogs on porcupine meat and firing at night on prowling wolves, he had made an uneventful trip back to the truck.

I enjoyed a good bath and a hearty meal that evening at the cabin of Armel Philipon. On Sunday afternoon, after another muddy trip from Dease Lake to Telegraph Creek, I again saw the welcome sight of my Detachment. I had been gone for 15 days and travelled 410 miles, 215 of which were on foot through rough country. I had lost 12 pounds and my feet did not heal for weeks.

Although we did not find Ford, it was established beyond reasonable doubt that he had met death, either from going through the treacherous spring ice, an accident, or being attacked by a bear or a moose. Philipon later found the skeletons of Ford's dogs near his main cabin. To this day, however, the fate of Hugh Ford remains unanswered. It is one more unsolved mystery, locked for ever in the vast expanse of Northern British Columbia.

MIKE: POLICE SLEIGH DOG

We dogs travelled the frigid wilderness for seven days without seeing another human or dog track, camped out at 50 below zero, and made round-trip winter journeys of 500 miles for mail. Tough, but all part of our duty.

by Corporal R. J. "Jack" Meek

I was born in August 1936 at remote McDames Creek Detachment in northwestern B.C., a region of stormy mountain peaks and nameless rivers. My mother was a beautiful Alsatian, leader of the police dog team, while a strapping huskie of over 100 pounds called Rum was my father. I had two brothers: Tony, black as the clouds which bring the Chinook winds and with ferocious gleaming yellow eyes, and Brownie, a cheerful robust sort, as tough as they come in that land of hard stubborn dogs. My sister, Lady, was given away to Bob Wilms, a placer-mining friend of the master, and we saw her quite often.

Our training began early for when we were two months old we started to shift for ourselves. We were fed boiled corn meal or rice, with fish meal or beef cracklings thrown in. When we were lucky we had a snowshoe rabbit to divide among us, or some fresh moose or caribou meat.

In February the weather settled down to clear skies, zero temperatures and soft dry snow. We were seven months old then and growing rapidly. So the boss, Constable Meek, caught us and put on collars for the first time.

Our education started by being led about at the end of the chain, then we were hooked up one to the other and walked around. Of course we'd often seen the other dogs of the Detachment setting off on a patrol with lots of noise and excitement. They came back several days or weeks later looking rather weary and not nearly so boisterous.

We were fitted with neck harness, which was to be our own, and one by one given turns at pulling with the big dogs.

On the last day of March 1937 we had our first patrol. It was from the Trading Post some 30 miles up McDames Creek to a mining camp, not far from where they said the largest gold nugget in B.C. was found in 1877.

We had a terribly difficult trip back to the Post. The ice had gone out of McDames Creek in places, and once we had to splash our way through swift flowing icy water up to our bellies. When we were safely on the other side my master very carefully dried our paws.

Opposite: This is me, Mike, photographed at McDames Creek in the early 1940s by Constable J. W. Purdy. His wife, Margaret, was the first white woman ever to feed or pet us.

We didn't get an opportunity to travel much more that winter as the snow melted rapidly. The ice went out on Dease River the first week in May and the Arctic summer commenced. We dogs didn't have a great deal to do during the summer, being tied up most of the time — though every few days we'd be let loose for a run.

The first boat from the Outside chugged gaily down to the Post towards the end of the first week in June and triggered excitement no end. Men were running about, shouting and talking till sunrise. The mail, oranges and eggs seemed to be popular.

Most dogs during the summer in B.C.'s Northland are outfitted with back packs for travel, tying in front and underneath the belly. Some dogs can carry as much as 50 pounds. In common with the other police dogs, we were fitted with side packs, but we never had a load much greater than 25 pounds.

In many ways summer travel with its long exciting days is more interesting than straining along narrow snow-bound winter trails. We usually walked along by ourselves, taking our own time, but when the big grizzlies were around we bunched close together right behind the master. The dangerous silvertips stayed way up high on the mountains most of the summer so we didn't often see or smell them.

The boss often travelled with Indians and we would hear them spinning yarns long after the evening meal. You couldn't say "into the night" because it never really got dark during summer. We loved walking through the northwoods during the lovely Arctic night. It was fresh and cool, mosquitoes never were quite as bad then and it somehow seemed to be much easier travelling. Moose and caribou fed during the cool of the twilight and we often saw them browsing in swamps and lakes, or on the thick moss of the hillsides.

We sometimes travelled to nearby lakes, both winter and summer, to haul in fish. Always a pleasant outing, it gave us a much appreciated bit of exercise.

Winter activity began by hauling firewood from a heavily timbered spot about a mile upstream. Five of us could haul a pretty heavy load with good going — from 500 to 700 pounds was average. Hauling wood was a chore but put us in shape for the long police patrols of the late winter.

Our first emergency job was to bring down a sick prospector named Dan Kean from way up McDames Creek. We were the first sleigh over the trail that winter which meant the Constable breaking trail every bit of the way. By this time we were becoming an efficient team, obeying Gee and Haw, Whoa and Mush with cheerful readiness. We learned how to swing wide at a sharp curve of the trail, how to keep well up on the bank of a river's center-sloping ice, to keep ahead of a sleigh going downhill in order not to get tangled harness, and how to keep warm on a bed of spruce boughs even on a bitterly cold night.

My first really long patrol occupied the entire month of March, during which time we travelled approximately 500 miles. With our boss, Constable Meek, and another white man we set out for Telegraph Creek early one morning, six of us dogs hooked to our best sleigh, a

Grizzlies and wolves always made us nervous. Here is a cabin after a grizzly decided to dine on some moose meat hanging inside.

Like Murphy, the stalwart fellow below, I spent an enjoyable summer wandering the woods with a prospector. Some dogs carried 50 pounds but we never had over 25.

return journey of some 500 wintery miles ahead of us. We acquired a brand new sleigh at Dease Lake, a sort of cross between a Yukon sleigh and a toboggan — in reality, a toboggan with low runners attached. We found it easier pulling, especially on soft snow — though there were only three of us to a sleigh now. Along the 70 odd miles between Dease Lake and Telegraph Creek large bands of caribou were roaming everywhere. The Constable shot a nice fat caribou and while we enjoyed some fresh meat they cached most of the carcass for the return journey. The meat was merely hoisted up a convenient dead spruce, well out of the reach of wolves, coyotes and such marauders.

We arrived at Telegraph Creek just as the last of the daylight faded, which was very early in the afternoon in that area. It was our first sight of a "town," even though the community consisted of mostly log buildings and about 200 people. There were lots of dogs, however. In fact many more than people. Seeing so many other dogs watching us we determinedly put on our best behavior and held our tails high. After all, we were the Police Team!

After a week's rest during which we saw hundreds of different kinds of canines including a rare little fellow known as a Tahltan Bear Dog , (now extinct) we felt quite refreshed. So our homeward trip was started with us chaps in excellent spirits. One unfortunate incident, however, marred the trip.

We were heading north right down the center of Dease Lake. It was a bright cloudless morning, the glaring spring sun in a cloudless sky reflected blindingly from acres and acres of ice and snow. We had bestirred ourselves early to get in a good day's travel and set off at a real smart clip. Our lead dog, Brownie, for some peculiar reason kept leading us off the trail, which was stupid, because the well beaten path was obvious. After the seventh or eighth time the boss went up and looked deep in Brownie's eyes. He was blind! Rest in a dark kennel is needed and the eyes will gradually regain their sight, but Brownie ever afterwards had a slight film over his eyes.

After two days rest for Brownie's benefit we set off down the Dease River for the Detachment. We made fast time as the men were becoming very skilful at making and breaking camp. They didn't use a tent in order to save weight, but simply erected a canvas windbreak which also served as the coverall for the sleigh. On both sleighs the men carried their axe and rifle ready to grab in an instant. A good axe seems to be the most important instrument a bushman owns. Some men use it exclusively and can make camp and have the meal cooking by its help in less than half an hour. The boss always carried several small moccasins for our feet, too. If the snow and ice became too rough for our much travelled paws, out would come the footgear. We didn't like them at first; tried to chew them off and all that, but found out how splendid they are for protecting the paws.

After a few day's rest at home we were off on another patrol — two teams of three dogs each, two men. This time we headed for the great North Country. The South Central Yukon has few trails and sometimes I thought we just travelled whichever route seemed easiest.

One afternoon we came over the brow of a hill. Beneath us lay a beautiful little lake surrounded by stately spruce and tamarack, while across the lake ran a well defined trail — the first one we'd seen since leaving the Post. In a moment we swept enthusiastically upon it. To my surprise it was a wolf trail, beaten wide and flat by a thousand feet.

We often heard timber wolves at night and at one camp they howled around us nearly all night. Early next morning we stumbled upon a young, freshly killed moose not 200 yards from camp.

That was the wildest country I'd ever seen. As we crossed valleys and clambered over mountain ranges, we were sometimes forced to double-up — taking one sleigh up a steep hillside at a time — with all the dogs and both men straining their utmost. For seven days we travelled without seeing a human track or habitation. The eighth day we made an extremely long pull — some 60 miles — and arrived at remote Lower Post on the Liard River late in the evening.

We returned to the Home Detachment by a different route, following Dease River all the way. With warm weather approaching, the river showed black, dangerous water in many places, while along the shore the ice slanted treacherously downwards, necessitating a rope tied to the sleigh held by a man on the river bank. In places we were forced to take to the dense spruce forests along the shore, and as much of the snow had melted it was very tough travelling. At one dangerous place we had to cross open water on a makeshift bridge of trees felled on the spot and placed from the bank across to river ice. We dogs made the tricky crossing one at a time, then the sleigh was carefully inched across by us fellows pulling at a safe distance from the end of a rope.

The weather was very mild — in fact our last day on the trail it rained buckets — but we didn't mind getting wet. We splashed across streams overflowing the ice several inches, but finally made the warm safety of our kennels after the 300-mile patrol.

Our last job that winter was to "rawhide" a moose out of the bush for a prospector. The kill was deep in the silent forests, about a mile away from the river, the artery of all travel. To prepare the "rawhide" the animal was butchered, the hide wrapped around the meat, some 800 to 1,000 lbs., the skin was then laced up and a tie made to the neck of the hide and to which we were hooked. The load is very flexible, it slithers over all the little bumps and valleys. As the hair is turned the proper way, it slides very easily. In fact in heavy bush country it is the only way to take out such a big animal as a moose.

I had a real break just at the beginning of summer. Instead of being tied up at the Detachment most of the time like the others, I went out into the hills with a splendid Norwegian named Johann Vollaug. We roamed the hills and prospect holes all summer while I carried his pack. The vigorous moving life was just to my liking and I learned many of the tricks of packing.

We started back on the old grind of hauling wood in November. Tiring, but better than hanging around in a kennel all day — besides, they fed us more when we worked. Occasionally we took a run out to

Constable Purdy and our patrol of 1942-43 amidst wilderness near Lower Post. The second team was driven by the Constable's wife, Margaret. In that vast empty land on some patrols for days we didn't see another human track.

one of the nearby lakes, hauling back fish which the men caught with nets through the ice.

The master was preparing to leave the Detachment soon, so many people came in from all the country round to say good-bye during the Christmas season of 1938. Christmas Day dawned at 45 degrees below zero, but seven white men and over 25 Indians and dozens of dogs gathered together at the Post to celebrate. It was the most exciting time we'd ever experienced at McDames Creek. On January 22, 1939, a big aeroplane took out the master. As the plane circled above us we said "Klahowya Tyee" — good-bye Chief — and turned to begin a new life under his successor, Jerry Davis.

Our first task under the new regime was a distasteful one — bringing in a body for burial. Poor old Dan Kean, struggling through his declining years all alone in a filthy little cabin some 30 miles from the Post, had finally mushed to the Happy Hunting Grounds. It was the third time our sleigh had been used as a catafalque and I hoped it would be the last. A couple of days later we sadly hauled our grisly load to the secluded graveyard at McDames Creek.

The "long patrol" of that winter came a bit later than usual. February and March are the very best months for travel in the Cassiar, though good conditions — a slight fall of soft dry snow on glare ice is perfect — often occur right up until the first week in May. It was March, however, before we left on the long wilderness journey to Lower Post. But we were caught in an unexpected spring thaw and stayed at the Post only overnight before heading home.

The sun shone as brightly as mid-summer, temperatures soared, and long stretches of open water told us the "in-between seasons" had arrived. These occupy about three weeks every spring and some two weeks in the fall. During those periods snow is too patchy and ice isn't

84

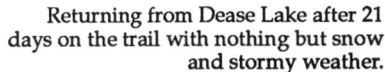
My brother, Tony, victim of our
unfortunate fight.

Returning from Dease Lake after 21
days on the trail with nothing but snow
and stormy weather.

strong enough for sleigh travel, while overland it's too muddy on the
primitive trails.

Cussing the unseasonable weather, Constable Davis was forced to
abandon our sleigh and we took to the woods and slippery game trails.
We were pretty gaunt when we got back and not in the best of humor.

Guess that's a poor excuse for the tragedy that happened next, but
the north is not a country of genteel manners or mild tempered dogs.
I don't know how it started, but I do know it was quite accidental.

My brother, Tony, and I always owned adjoining kennels. During
one warm spring night, we were both gazing at the moon and moving
about. Then it happened. A careless move, a tangled chain, a warning
growl and then we were at each other's throats. Blood and hair flew
high, while the rest of the dogs joined in the ferocious clamor. In a few
minutes poor, dear, misunderstood Tony lay dying in the mud and
snow. I still carry several scars from that terrible night, and they're not
all on my hide.

After that unfortunate death duel, summer slipped quietly away.
In the winter of 1940-41 we set out on a routine patrol to the Liard River
country. The outward trip was fine, a young man named Frank Moon
travelling with us for the patrol. Setting off on the return trip from
Lower Post under good conditions we had mushed some 10 miles

when fine dry snow started whirling about us, cutting visibility to 100 yards. Normally that wouldn't have bothered us, but when the temperature started dropping with an increasing wind, it wasn't so pleasant. Conditions worsened — deep snow, an unbroken trail, biting headwinds and terribly slow, heavy going. At last we were forced to hole up at French Creek, about half way home.

Still it snowed and snowed some more! Grub ran short and, crouched on a bed of spruce boughs, we could do nothing but wait. A whole week passed before we were able to set forth into a cold strange world. Not a track nor a sign of life anywhere except an occasional snowshoe rabbit — creatures upon which we were forced to live.

In the meantime the few residents of McDames Creek were getting very concerned over our continued absence — especially during the bitter storm. Just as the third week of our patrol passed, we laboriously crept into the Detachment, lean and hungry.

Then, in its glorious way, summer came once more to the Cassiar and quickly passed. On September 9, 1941, came another change when two chechakos (newcomers) landed from the river boat. We learned they were Constable J. W. Purdy and his wife, Margaret. She was the first white woman ever to feed or pet us. We dogs didn't know what to think of her at first, and hid in our kennels whenever she approached. But every morning after breakfast she fed us leftover pancakes. It didn't take long before she was immensely popular with all of us.

Two novelties awaited us that winter. First, we made a patrol upriver with the new man on November 18, earliest in my experience. Secondly, we started pulling a 10-foot toboggan instead of the conventional Yukon sleigh. In fresh snow and through heavy brush it was certainly easier pulling, but not so good on icy trails.

One time we were jogging up the Dease on a lone patrol when we saw as strange a scene as I've ever experienced. I was amazed to find the entire surface covered with a great herd of caribou. Even way up on the hillsides we could see the migrating animals.

They hurried on, not stopping even when we approached to within 20 or 30 feet of them. In fact some of the larger bulls became quite threatening, lowering their magnificent heads, snorting and pawing. Personally, I'm more afraid of their front hoofs which can strike with the speed of summer lightning. A gun fired over their heads a couple of times opened a lane for the team through which we dodged.

At Porter's Landing, a wee hamlet on the northern extremity of Dease Lake, we discovered the lake had frozen over just the night before. As conditions next morning were perfect, we set off down the 24-mile stretch to Lake House at the southern extremity. Since the ice was thin and kept cracking underneath us we stepped lively — so lively in fact, we covered the distance in three hours 20 minutes, over seven miles per hour.

We stayed at Lake House a couple of days. During our stay we found the men very excited and much war talk going on. Once we heard someone shout "War is declared on the Japs by the States."

The boss wanted to be home for Christmas, so we pulled our best and arrived there with two days to spare. We were rewarded by his gracious wife with extra pancakes and double helpings of rice and cornmeal.

The following summer we enjoyed a good long rest, though I must say I preferred packing through the hills and mountains. Camping in a clump of jackpines or beside a dashing icy stream with the smell of pine smoke and man food has something about it which gets in your blood.

November 1942 started with a cold spell. The river froze and it looked like good travelling so in the second week of that month we set out for Dease Lake, about 75 miles away. The Constable had his wife with him, and a capable dog-musher she was, too. She had a team of new dogs for herself and carried the dog feed on a slightly smaller toboggan than ours.

No sooner had we set out when the weather turned soft and warm. First it started to rain, making the toboggan pretty sticky pulling. Gradually the rain turned to sleet and we splashed and strained and slipped until almost everyone was played out.

Then the weather turned really cold with flurries of snow. On the 50-mile stage to Porter's Landing we ran into every type of poor condition. The Constable broke trail every step of the way. We struggled against high drifting piles of it, loose bottomless trails, overflow and cruel freezing winds that made you inhale quick shallow breaths. It took us a week to mush that 50 miles — seven miles a day. By contrast, the year before we had made seven miles an hour on our trip down Dease Lake.

Three days later, feeling quite refreshed and determined to be home for Christmas, we pulled out of Porter's Landing and headed down the Dease. The cold weather and drifting snow made the whole valley an undulating sheet of unbroken whiteness. So began the heartbreaking task of tramping out a trail again. Slow going it was, too, often the boss had to retrace his steps due to overflow or an impassable situation. Of the many trips up and down the Dease that was the worst of all.

The following summer we were moved to Lower Post where there was all sorts of activity. The Alaska Highway was changing the tempo of the whole North Country. When we first visited Lower Post some six or seven years before, it was the most isolated spot you could wish for. And now — why they even had buses and jeeps at the Post. Noisy things with the stink of gasoline on 'em.

In the winter of 1943-44 Constable Purdy came ever-so-close to drowning. We were on patrol again. The going was pretty good, about eight inches of soft snow covering Blue River — a large tributary of the Dease. We'd completed a trapline check and were heading for home, following a trail downstream. All was going well, then the boss paused to fix his snowshoe harness. We continued on the trail, going round a curve of the river.

Out of the corner of my eye I could see the Constable cutting

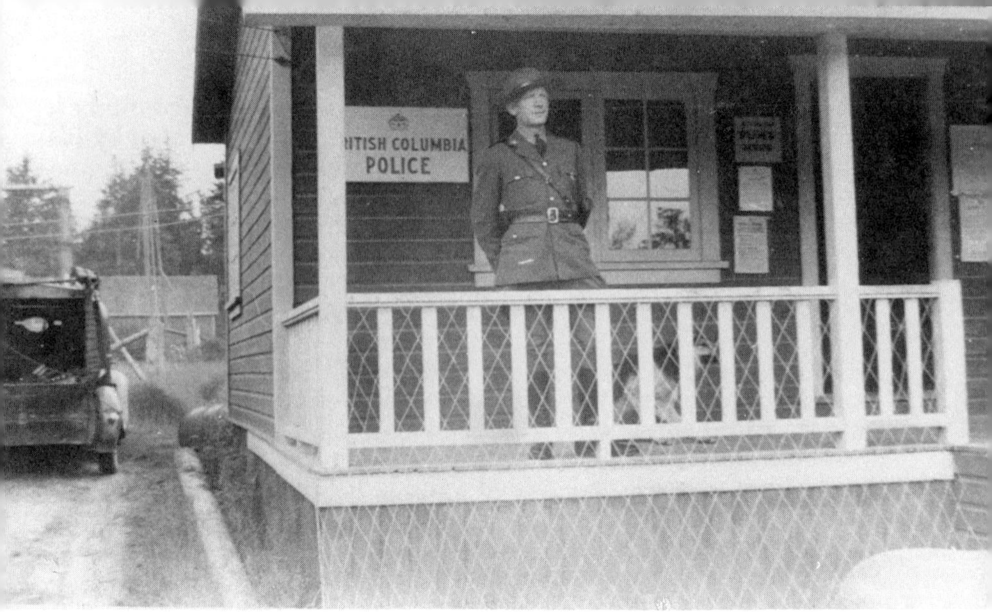
ITISH COLUMBIA
POLICE

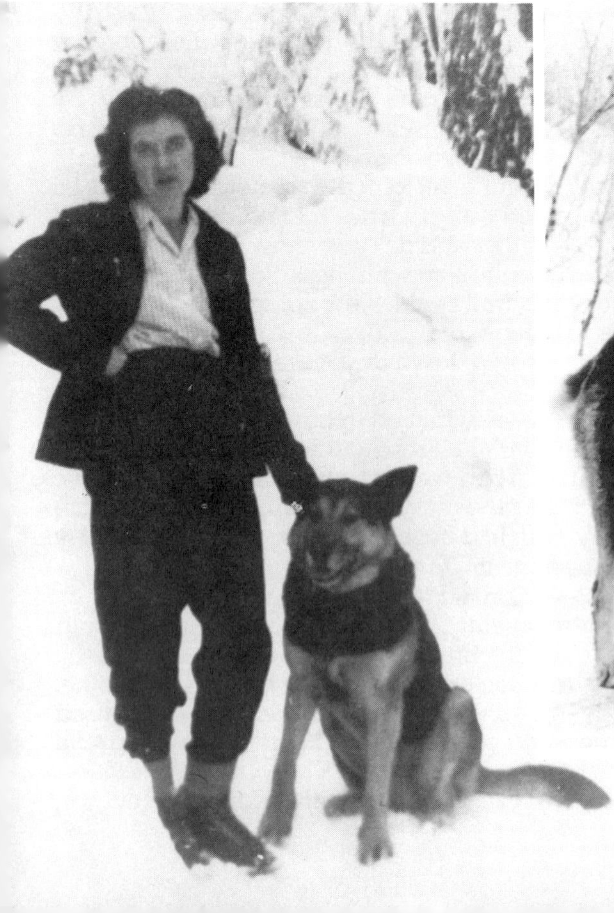

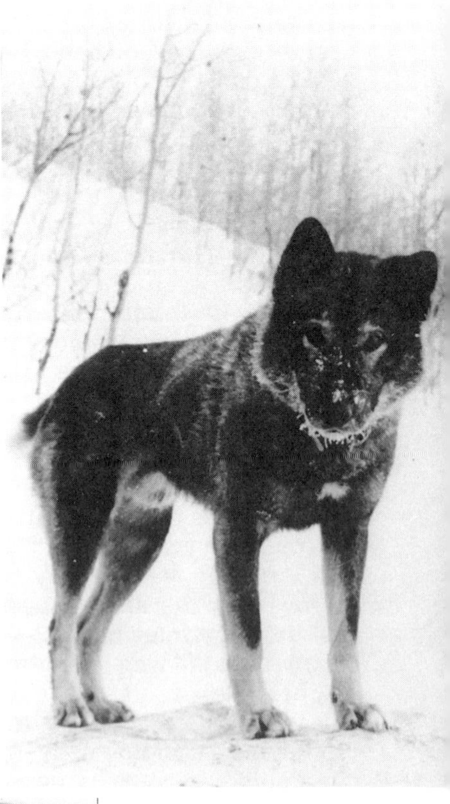

straight across unbroken snow to catch up to us. I knew he shouldn't have done it. I could anticipate trouble — and sure enough it came. River snow can be very deceptive, with open water just under the surface. That's just what the master walked into. In a second he crashed into black rushing water.

Now when you travel with a toboggan you always have a long rope dangling behind for controlling the load on a sharp hill or a side-hill or some sort of emergency. I saw the boss make a grab for the rope and clutch it like a drowning person. Then he yelled at us one single word: "Mush!"

As far as I was concerned he didn't need to yell. I could see the whole thing coming up, so I put my head down and pulled for all I was worth. The other chaps had paused when they heard the shout and turned around in confusion. But I know a good boss when I have one, so put all I had into it. The water must have been dragging greedily to pull him under the ice for it took all my strength — and I'm no pup — to win an inch. Then the other boys in the team saw our predicament and threw themselves into the harness.

Slowly we surged ahead, feet slipping, lungs bursting and harness as taut as a wire. Snowshoes were almost the boss's undoing as the swift gurgling waters clutched and writhed around him — dragging him under the impassive unchanging snow. The long Cassiar type snowshoe impeded his violent struggles to get free of the ice. But with our frenzied efforts, the toboggan finally heaved ahead, hauling the master out on safe ice.

Streaking for a clump of trees he quickly dug matches from the sleigh and somehow got a fire going. Then in the sub-zero cold he took off his now freezing clothes and got into his eiderdown. We lay in the snow patiently. He was up all night drying his clothes and the following day we resumed the trip, none the worse.

That autumn, Constable Purdy was replaced by Constable Faryon, and so Brownie and I went out to Burns Lake Detachment in Central B.C. Here we stayed for quite a few months.

That winter there was an epidemic of distemper amongst the dogs and unfortunately Brownie contracted the disease. He lay for over a month fighting for his life while Constable Purdy and his wife gave him every care possible — sometimes far into the night. But, alas, Brownie never recovered. He lies in an honored grave near the police quarters there. As fine a chum as dog ever had.

Eventually the boss was transferred to North Vancouver and I was put on pension. I'm quite content to bask in the sun and dream of adventures in the far away Cassiar.

The police dog team which saved Constable Purdy's life. Mike
is between the shafts, Brownie in the lead.

In the preceding article, police sleigh dog Mike
described the near tragedy when his master plunged
through the ice of the Blue River. Here is Constable
John W. "Jack" Purdy's account of

CLOSER TO GOD THAN I'VE EVER BEEN

In August 1941, while stationed at Powell River, I was what might be
termed "shanghaied" from the B.C. Game Department and posted to
McDames Creek near the Yukon boundary. I accepted the transfer
without fully realizing the hardships I was to endure in the North
where I was to perform both the duties pertinent to the Game Department and the Provincial Police from 1941 to 1946.

I married on a Saturday night and left immediately with my bride from Vancouver, travelling by a Union Steamships' vessel to Wrangel, Alaska. From there we went by Barrington Transportation up the Stikine River to Telegraph Creek, then over a 73-mile stretch from that point by truck to Dease Lake, thence by river boat from the head of the lake to McDames Creek. What a three-week honeymoon that was for a new bride!

In the winter of 1942 illness overtook my wife. By use of the Hudson's Bay Company's radio at McDames Creek I had an airplane (a Junkers flown by the late Russ Baker) come from Prince George to convey her and me to Watson Lake. Here she boarded the old Yukon Southern airline for Vancouver.

During that winter, through loneliness, I spent as much time as possible on patrol with my dog team. One of those expeditions took me north from McDames Creek to cover the trapline of William Tsgar (pronounced "Cigar") who had his main cabin on the Blue River which empties into the Dease. He was reportedly taking beaver out of season. My only guide was a map which told me roughly where I was. I struck his trapline trail just north of Coolihan Canyon on the Dease River and found it had about eight inches of snow on it. I was forced to break trail ahead of the dogs.

It was a practice in that country when encountering such conditions to bring your dally line — a 50-foot length of rope attached to the curl of the toboggan — back to the handlebars and fasten it so it was taut. The taut rope formed a slight curve in the bottom of the toboggan, assisting in manoeuvring a crooked course around trees.

I had been travelling over two days and expected to hit the Blue River some time during the next. I noticed as I was breaking trail that my right snowshoe tie had become undone, so I let the dogs go on bucking the snow while I was securing my snowshoe. I checked the other and also found its tie loose. I had previously noticed that the dally line had become unfastened and was dragging alongside the toboggan, but decided to leave it since it was about 2:30 p.m. and soon be time to make camp. As it transpired, it was lucky that I made that decision.

When I was ready to get going again the dogs had disappeared. At first I thought they had gone down into a swale and would soon appear on the rise of its other side, and ran to catch up. Then I discovered they had come to the Blue River and made a turn downstream.

I should explain that as winters in the North progress, the water freezes to the bottom of rivers and causes pressure on the ice, wearing it away completely in places and making it paper thin in others. As I reached the river bank I decided to overtake the dogs by taking a shortcut over the ice of a bay in the stream. It was one of the thin spots which was covered with snow, but which the team had sensed and avoided. I plunged through.

I don't know whether I touched bottom or not because the shock of the cold water was so great. However, I must have let out a yell because the dogs stopped. Just out of my reach at the edge of the hole in which I floundered was the trailing dally line. The pressure of the river's current against my well secured snowshoes began to pull me under the ice which crumbled as my fingers clawed at the edge of the hole. I realized I was losing the battle to scramble to thicker ice. Many thoughts ran through my mind in short time. My first was of my wife, and then that I would probably drown. I thought of the dogs — how they might tangle in the brush and starve to death.

I knew that my only chance of survival was to somehow grasp the dally line. I took a gamble and made a lunge for the rope. Although I had swallowed water, by a miracle I managed to seize it and made a turn about my wrist. Then I shouted at the dogs. Fortunately, my shaft dog, Mike, didn't require much urging. He took up the slack just enough to keep me from going under. I began to scream at the dogs to pull. When they commenced I thought my arm was going to come out of its socket. Finally, I began to slip out of the hole. The dogs dragged me a good 75 yards through the snow before they stopped.

I knew full well that it would not be long before my water-drenched clothing would be frozen to my body. About 300 yards down river was a patch of timber and I ran for it as fast as I could. But to reach the spot was more of a climb from the river than the dogs could manage. I grabbed the lead dog by his collar and assisted the team to the wooded area, literally dragging them behind me.

I immediately unleashed the coverall of the toboggan and obtained a large box of matches. Breaking twigs and gathering squaw grass I tried to light a fire. But my hands were so numb I couldn't feel whether I held a match or not. It was then the terrible fear of death came upon me. Had I escaped drowning only to perish for want of a fire?

I frantically grabbed a handful of matches, scraped them on the side of the box, and they ignited. I thrust them under the pile of twigs and heaved a sigh of relief as they burst into flame.

Then came the ordeal of taking off my clothes in the sub-zero temperature and crawling into my sleeping robe because I didn't have a change of clothing with me. All night long I hobbled around in the robe, gathering anything I could that would burn to keep the fire replenished. Hanging on a pole between two trees were my wet garments, scorching on one side and freezing on the other. As I kept the weather records for the Meteorological Station at Victoria, I was required to carry the maximum and minimum thermometers, together with the weather record book in my grub box. I was aware it was -32°F.

It was a continuous routine all night, turning my clothes and adding fuel to the fire while I was kept company by a little owl with his constant hooting.

That night I'm sure I was closer to God than I have ever been in my life. I wondered if the people of society realized how much we were giving of ourselves to keep them safe, or the terrible hardships faced by those who served amidst the hazardous and gruelling conditions of the harsh Cassiar winter.

BY THE BOOK

The policeman's life was governed by the B.C. Provincial Police General Orders and the Police Regulations. General Order Number #139 in January 1933 listed the value of clothing and equipment issued to each man:

Tunic	$ 19.10	Fur cap (winter)	$ 4.00
Breeches	12.00	Leather coat	25.00
Trousers	8.35	Gauntlets (leather)	2.85
Overcoat (pea jacket)	24.00		
Slicker (regular)	6.95	***Other Equipment***	
Slicker (cavalry style)	9.75	Sam Browne belt	5.00
Necktie	.84	Holster (leather)	1.50
Pair high boots (Strathcona)	11.50	Handcuff pouch (leather)	1.00
Peaked cap	2.85	Police badge (identification)	1.00
Cap cover	.85	1 pair handcuffs	8.00
Stetson hat	8.50	Revolver	37.50
Leather band for Stetson	.50	Cap badge	1.50
Lanyard and swivel	1.85	1 set tunic buttons and badges	3.85
2 shirts (flannel w/collars	6.00	1 set overcoat buttons and badges	1.85
2 shirts (cotton, summer) w/collars.	5.00	Goggles (motorcycle)	6.00
Pair hip rubber boots	5.00		

Item 61 in the B.C. Provincial Police Regulations noted: "Every member of the Force will be required to have his uniform altered to fit, and to keep same in order at his own expense."

The policemen could wear Oxfords if they chose -— but had to buy them.

Item 73 listed the 1937 pay scale:

Minimum per month		*Maximum per month*	
Commissioner	$ 335.00		$ 400.00
Assistant Commissioner	275.00		300.00
Inspector	208.33		250.00
Sub-Inspector	190.00		225.00
Paymaster	175.00		200.00

Rate per Day

Staff Sergeants	$ 5.00	2nd Class Constables	$ 3.55
Sergeants	4.75	3rd Class Constables	3.30
Corporals	4.30	Probationers	3.00
Detectives	4.30	Special Constables	3.50
1st Class Constables	3.80		

On the average, Constables of the B.C. Provincial Police were promoted to Corporals after 12 years, and to Sergeant after about another four years. The rule wasn't absolute. Some bright boys did better, but then there's always an exception.

RED LIGHTS AT PRINCE RUPERT

The city fathers permitted the girls to go downtown only on Tuesdays, they were medically examined once a month, and it wasn't unusual to see prominent businessmen doff their hats to some of them.

by 1st Class Constable Balfour E. "Bal" Munkley

When I joined the B.C. Provincial Police in 1938 my first assignment was to B.C.'s northcoast city of Prince Rupert. There I learned that the city had a full-blown red-light district that city officials wanted to be in operation. Since we were policing the community under contract, wishes of city fathers were an integral part of such contracts.

Reasons that the red-light district was condoned were that Prince Rupert was a seaport and also the center of a very active fishing industry engaging not only those who brought in the catches, but those who processed them in the canneries. Both conditions, as well as others, attracted a rough element. The red-light district was thought to be a safeguard against offences that could be fully expected unless there was such a means of deterrent.

The district, known as "over the hump," was located on the far side of a high hill separating it from the main part of the city, isolated from what was defined as the residential area. Prince Rupert at that time had no highway connecting it to the outside world, with the result that many people did not own cars and relied on a large fleet of taxis for transportation. Since the street leading to "over the hump" ran past the police station, we had first-hand knowledge of how well the taxi business flourished.

There were about 40 girls in possibly a dozen houses. In order to exercise control over their inmates, the madams kept the police informed of the arrivals and departures. When a new girl hit town, her madam would arrange for her appearance before a magistrate to enter a plea of guilty to being an inmate of a "disorderly house," upon which she was fined $25. The conviction was a definite influence against risking a second, as a repeat carried a very severe penalty. This practice was literally a club held over a girl's head to ensure her good behavior. Without doubt, the madams controlled their girls with a firm hand.

The city officials laid down rules for the girls. They were not permitted downtown except on Tuesdays, when during the afternoon they might patronize dress shops and make other purchases, and in the evening attend the local theatre where they sat segregated in loges. It was not unusual to see prominent citizens doff their hats to some of the girls, and no one seemed to think this action amiss. Other than

Opposite: Prince Rupert's first police
office and courthouse in 1908.

The Prince Rupert City Detachment in 1938. Standing, from left: Constable W. J. Currie, Constable D. D. McIndoe, the author, Constable A. P. L. Cartwright. Sitting, left to right: Constable J. Lockie, Sergeant C. C. Jacklin, Constable J. W. Todd.

Tuesdays, one never saw a prostitute on the streets. Therefore there was no soliciting.

Once a month the girls were required to have a medical examination and bring the certificate to the police office as proof. I was stationed in Prince Rupert for two years and I never heard of a single case of venereal disease traceable to "the hump." Doctors have argued with me since that the inmates of the red-light houses could have been infected for most of the month following their examination. Nevertheless, I still feel that the procedure of the inspections cut down the odds very significantly, compared with today's situation when no examinations are performed.

The operation of "the hump" was not entirely confined to the oldest profession. Social evenings with drinking and dancing were also part of the routine, conducted with what could be termed integrity. I have spoken to many a single fisherman who went to the district for an evening carrying a large sum of money. He would awaken in the morning, his pockets empty and no idea who had taken his cash, where he had been or what he had done. The madam, however, would present him with a detailed statement covering his activities and the balance of his money after the bill had been paid. It was often in the range of $1,500. To me that was a goodly sum since I was getting $3 a day, less deductions.

The crime rate within the red-light district was practically nil, although one girl had been murdered prior to my arrival at Prince Rupert. On the occasions when our duties required us to go "over the hump," our knocks on doors resulted in cordial invitations to enter. None of the customers appeared even slightly embarrassed by us seeing them with the girls, despite the fact that some of them were as likely as not persons of importance in the city.

Closure of "the hump" came shortly after the outbreak of World War Two when Prince Rupert became a garrison town. Some of the troops contracted venereal disease and because of pressure of the military the shutdown was ordered. I was advised by one of the local doctors that the source of infection was a number of "non-professional" girls who moved into the city following the troops.

While the line was operating I knew of not a single case of rape or indecent assault, but all hell broke loose when the closure was effected. The operation, as it had been, precluded any local girls being procured by pimps, and all the girls were imported.

I remember one madam (Blanche Hunt) who passed away in her 80s. She had one of the largest funerals in Prince Rupert's history!

REMINISCENCES OF A FRONTIER POLICEMAN

For 16 years from 1896 he was the only policeman from
Quesnel north some 600 miles to the Yukon border,
and west over 400 miles from the Rocky
to the Coast Mountains.

by Constable David H. Anderson

I joined the B.C. Provincial Police in the summer of 1896 and in August
of that year was sent to Quesnel in the Northern Cariboo. There were
very few Constables in the country. So far as I know I was the first to
be stationed in Quesnel, which was only a small place with a few
families living in it and not many in the district around.

There were Constables at Richfield near Barkerville, Quesnel
Forks, Clinton, 150 Mile House, Ashcroft and Lillooet. They were
spread very thin with most of them 50 to 75 miles apart. Fortunately,
people were generally peaceful with respect for the law.

I had some hard cases to deal with at times but I never took a bluff.
I didn't care if a prisoner was as big as a house, even if he was John L.

Constable Anderson outside Quesnel's jail and courthouse in the early 1900 s.
Here he brought murderer Charley Benton and held him for over a week.

Sullivan himself. If I had to take him, I took him. I could always get lots of help if I needed it to follow or track a man. For tracking I could also fall back on Indians, who cannot be bettered for that work. I covered my district on horseback for the greater part of the year, and in winter on snowshoes or with dogs. I went up to Stuart Lake (an over 300-mile round trip) on one case with two Special Constables when we had to break our way through with two feet of snow on the ground. At one time I used to get an allowance for my horse for five months of the year, $17 a month, but that didn't last long.

In addition to hunting for offenders, we were called upon to do a lot of things which never got into reports and for which we never asked, or got, any credit. We settled lots of little difficulties between neighbors and we did a lot to prevent bad feeling that would have been created by people brooding over petty spats and jealousies. Disputes between neighbors that in a city are soon forgotten because there is so much more to occupy attention, in the country get magnified, and in some cases end in crimes.

In settling anything like that a Constable is really doing only his ordinary duty as a peace officer. In cases of accident we were often called in to arrange for getting the victims to hospital and, as there were no ambulances, it was sometimes difficult to get them there without too much jolting. The Cariboo Road was always in fair condition, but most of the side roads and farm roads were bad. Often a person had to be brought out over a trail.

Those were the days when towns and bars were wide open, with no limit to the hours of sale except for Sunday interval from 11:00 o'clock on Saturday night until 1 o'clock Monday morning.

At any hour of the other six days you could get a drink, but as a matter of fact there would not be much doing in the early morning hours. The hotels in Quesnel when I arrived were the Occidental, the Cariboo and the Armstrong. The Occidental was a four-storey building and the Cariboo was three storey. They were both good hotels, comfortable and well conducted. The bar was along the left hand side and open to the dining room as well, what would nowadays be called a lobby.

There was generally a crowd around the bar and at times a good sized crowd at that. Two bits a drink was the price. If a miner came in from Barkerville or the other mining camps, it was the custom of the country that he stand drinks for the crowd. When I first came, there was usually a game of draw poker going on and sometimes two or three of them. Stakes were pretty high at times. But in 1899 a stop was put to gambling in bars and the old-timers were pretty sore about it for a while. They thought it an invasion of British liberty and all that. The older men as a rule played solo or euchre for the drinks, not for money.

There was very little trouble in any of the hotels. If a man began to get quarrelsome the proprietor or bartender would put him out or, if he was staying at the house, lock him in his room until he sobered up. There was a general regard for the law, and when a Constable said

The Cariboo and the Occidental Hotels in Quesnel with a six-horse stagecoach in the late 1890s. Both hotels were destroyed in a fire during World War One.

something they paid attention to him. But there were exceptions.

My old Stetson hat shows a clean cut bullet hole through the crown within an inch of my brain. It was at Four Mile Creek above Quesnel that it happened. I was riding along on my customary patrol, looking for an Indian who was wanted, when a bullet pierced my hat. I jumped off my horse, threw the lines down, and dashed into the bushes. Out of the corner of my eye I noticed where the trunks of two cottonwoods were cut by the bullet. I pulled out my gun and dived in.

When a second shot did not come I knew it was no white man. It took me some little time but I had the satisfaction of getting Mr. Indian and, later on, of seeing him sent up for attempted murder.

The hardest men, the "hard boiled" ones as they call them nowadays, are the best to handle. They make better prisoners than the sneaky, cut-throat class, the devils who'll do you in the dark. The "hardest" man I ever had was Charley Phillips, alias Benton. Although he was from the U.S., he had done time in Kamloops and New Westminster jails for rape. At the latter place he met Charley Rose, a Cariboo half-breed. They struck up an acquaintance that served Phillips afterward and led to my confrontation with him.

After being released in B.C., Phillips went to Seattle. Here he got into trouble with the police and ended up murdering Patrolman Wells who was taking him to jail. Phillips was re-captured but had his right hand shot off. He served 12 years for the murder before escaping.

He went back to his old stamping ground along the boundary

between Washington and British Columbia. He knew every foot of that country, all the trails, and the Indians and half breeds sheltered and shielded him, some from sympathy and others from fear. But even the ones that gave him shelter through fear were not likely to inform on him, so he had little to be scared of. The few white settlers in that part of the State had little to do with him for he was looked upon as an ugly customer and was known to be a dead shot. A good deal of his trouble then, as it had been earlier, came from eyeing somebody else's wife or girl.

Amongst others he fell foul of was Marshal Ralph Siebert. One day Siebert was driving in a wagon with a neighbor when they met Charley riding horseback with a rifle across his saddle. As soon as Siebert saw Charley he jumped down from the wagon and tried to get away. But his clothes caught in a barbed wire fence. As he stuck there struggling Charley rode up and shot him dead.

Charley, who went by the name of Benton at this time, was a great horseman. The same night he was across the bridge at Ashcroft and he looked up Charley Rose in Cariboo and stayed with him in hiding.

In Chilcotin he hung around between Meldrum and Riske Creeks in order to see a young half-breed girl that he was sweet on. He was always a devil after women. After being there for some time he had some trouble with Charley Rose over his attentions to Charley's wife, and he moved on. We then got word that he was coming in the direction of Quesnel.

I got six good men and had them sworn in as Specials. I put two of them to watch on Telegraph Creek, two on Baker Creek, and I took

Constable David Anderson, center in the back row, with the Quesnel District Rifle Association he was instrumental in organizing. An excellent shot, he won many trophies. The Anderson Shield became a coveted award and today hangs in the Clubhouse at the Quesnel Rod and Gun Club.

two men, Frank E. Aiken with a rifle and Fred Curtis with a repeating shotgun, to where he had left the trail. Benton had a horse with a broken hoof so that it was no trouble tracking him. I spent two anxious hours in the moonlight trailing him. We knew he would have no compunction shooting any or all of us if he could. We found him eventually and got the drop on him in a hollow where he had stopped to rest his horses. He was somewhat surprised because he had counted on getting into the wilds of northern Chilcotin ahead of any pursuit. "Lift that left hand good and high," I shouted, "higher still."

I had to keep him over a week in Quesnel jail waiting for a stage. The stage didn't go farther than Soda Creek, so I had to sleep with him there the first night out. "Allow me to tell you that I take any chance I can get," he told me. I told him that I took no chance; that I would take him down and he could make up his mind to that. The American authorities wanted him sent down under heavy guard. Superintendent Hussey told them the man who was bringing him down was all the guard needed. I felt quite proud when I heard our old chief had said that.

We only got to 150 Mile the next night and I turned him over to Constable Yolland, who wanted to put a heavy guard on him. I said, "I don't care what you do but I want a night's sleep tonight, and you be sure to turn him over to me in the morning." Yolland hired another man to keep him company walking around the jail all night. I got him down to the coast and turned him over. The Washington authorities put him in irons and with a guard of half a dozen officers armed to the teeth. I had a good laugh at them to myself.

In 1898 I had a big bronco which I called Mike. He was a fine horse and almost human. Then I picked up a mongrel dog around 150 Mile House. I named him Chummie and he was of great use to me. I would say, "All right, get him." Before the man knew where he was, Chummie would be on him.

A good horse and a good dog are about the best friends a man can have. You need a good horse when you are constantly on the go, mainly along trails. A good dog is not only company when a man is travelling alone but is of great assistance to a Constable, as Chummie was to me many a time.

During the Klondike rush I was up and down the trail (northwest of Quesnel) all the time, watching for and helping the unfortunate men who were taking the overland trail to the land of gold, as they called it. Very many of them had no idea at all what they were going to be up against. By the time they got to the Nechako River (in Central B.C.), lots of them were beginning to turn back disheartened and convinced that the road to the Klondike was not to be found by the overland route.

They were a reckless lot: could not light a fire or make camp properly, or secure the game that was so plentiful around them. They did not know how to pack a horse; in fact they did not know how to look after any pack animal. There were dead horses every two or three miles along the trails. Men had trouble rounding them up in the mornings. They got to be afraid of losing them, and after packing them hard all day tied them up short to a tree all night. No wonder they lost so many.

The hardships men underwent affected their tempers, as you could tell from casual things you would notice or hear about. There was an awful lot of petty bickering among members of parties, which flared into rows and fights sometimes. Men used to quarrel about the route they should take, when they should camp, where they should camp, who should look after this or that camp chore — cutting wood, or lighting the fire, or cooking, or attending to the horses — how far or how fast they had travelled.

In fact, there was not a single subject that men travelling in a party were likely to talk about but they would quarrel over. It goes to show what a frazzled state their tempers were in when they would let themselves go so easily. There is not a doubt that some of these disputes ended in killings which no one ever heard of.

You would think that if someone in a party you were with did not turn up or disappeared, you would make some inquiry as to what had become of him. But it didn't seem to worry any of these chaps at all. A man might have been killed or he might have got lost but they didn't put themselves to any trouble looking for him. We had some inquiries for people who had disappeared on the overland route but we were never able to do anything in regard to them. It was impossible to trace them in any way or even to tell for sure if they had ever passed that way.

One day I had crossed the Mud (Chilako) River on my way to a meeting-spot to get a fellow who was being brought down from the Omineca for trial. I met on the trail a big fellow, blunt and autocratic and domineering, who had charge of Sir Arthur Curtis' outfit. This fellow was called Pocock. He was supposed to be a great frontiersman, traveller and guide, but he had a lot to learn about travelling in this country. "Did you see Sir Arthur?" says he.

"Sir who?" says I.

Then he tells me about this outfit and Sir Arthur going out to hunt for the horses, and they waiting awhile for him. As he didn't come back they went on to Bobtail Lake.

"The hell you did," says I. "Do you mean to tell me that when a man gets lost you don't look for him? Come on back and let's see if we can find him."

Pocock and Sir Arthur had had a quarrel, which may explain why he didn't bother about his absence. The party kept military camp and more or less military discipline, and each one had to do his share of the camp chores.

Sir Arthur was a pretty high-spirited and proud man and insisted on doing his share of the chores. This morning he was to go after the horses at daybreak. The horses came drifting in in small groups but Sir Arthur never appeared. As mentioned, they left him lost in the bush without making any effort to organize a search.

I was not able to wait very long myself, as I was due at my meeting place, but we went back to the Curtis camp, rode around a bit and shouted and fired several shots without getting any response. Of course this was a good many hours after and Curtis had probably wandered a long way by that time. The Hudson's Bay Company went to great expense to look for him with Indian trackers when the matter was reported and his friends in England had written the heads of the Company in London to order a search, but that was some few days later.

I heard that they only gave one day's ration at a time to the Indians hunting for him. Leon, a Stony Creek Indian, was in charge of the party. He said to me afterwards: "Anderson, they just give us enough for one day. If they gave me a week's provisions I would have got him. This man just go like one crazy bear."

A chap told me that he had camped on Bednesti Lake, half way between Mud River and Chilako, and there was a strange human cry at night. This was about the time Sir Arthur would have reached that neighborhood if headed in that direction. There was a big swamp between this chap and the direction from which the cry came. I have no doubt that poor Curtis had been wandering in the bush, and that he quite likely foundered in the swamp. There was some talk of murder when the story came out, but it is certain that there was nothing in it. They never found any trace of him although they found one or two places where he had evidently been.

Frank Aiken and I spent three weeks in the Chilcotin country after Ernest Louis, an Indian who, with a companion, killed a Chinaman for $5 and a plug of tobacco. We gradually rounded him up and kept driving him before us until we had got him on the east side of the Fraser River. Then I sent a telegram to headquarters with directions where and when to send good men. They acted on my directions, with the result that they dropped on Louis according to schedule.

One time it was reported to me that there was a crazy Indian on a rancherie who was threatening to kill any other Indian who approached. James Deacon and I went down and found a tremendous big and powerful man spreading terror among his neighbors. He was six feet four inches tall, and to his natural strength was added the strength and cunning of insanity. He was standing at his door and taking shots at any Indian who appeared. We rushed him and had an awful struggle. He nearly got the better of us a few times but we hung on. I broke my baton over his head without it making much appreciable difference, and finally Deacon shot him. He would have done for both of us if we had not done so, as his strength did not appear to lessen and we were getting exhausted.

I could keep going for a week with stories of the things that have happened during my years in the Provincial Police service.

(In 1912 Constable Anderson left the police force. He became a partner with building contractor Harry Joyce and they erected many of Quesnel's buildings. One of them, the United Church, still stands. Afterward he settled on a farm at Dragon Lake some three miles east of Quesnel. Here he built a log home which is still used. He farmed until his death in 1940 at 78.)

MEMORABLE "BEAKS" AND OTHER JUSTICES

Provincial Policemen had many memorable
experiences with the "Beak" — local Magistrates and
others who presided over court. Here are a few,
including three fearless gold-rush judges.

UNFLAPPABLE BARNEY MULVANEY
by G. W. "Andy" Anderson

Most of the Stipendiary Magistrates during the B.C. Provincial Police
era served the province well, even though the majority were ordinary
laymen from all walks of life. Knowledge of the law was not a qualifica-
tion for their appointment, but, as a rule, with good common sense and
the coaching of the members of the Force, they fulfilled the respon-
sibilities of their offices capably and impartially. At times, however,
many were unpredictable.

I cherish the association I had with one in particular. In 1947-48 I
was stationed at Burns Lake as a Constable under Bill Richmond.
Lyster "Barney" Mulvaney, about 70, was the Stipendiary Magistrate.
He was a bachelor and lived in town or at his small place several miles
south. On one occasion an Indian woman named "Sunshine Susie"
appeared before Barney, charged with creating a disturbance by fighting. Constable Richmond was prosecuting, and informed the court of
the circumstances. He then produced a large jackknife which he stated
was found in the accused's possession after her arrest.

When Barney saw the knife he showed keen interest. He rose from his seat, leaned over his desk and said to Susie, "Where did you get that knife?"

Susie looked him in the eye and replied, "You know, Barney. You gave it to me the night you stayed with me in my shack!"

Sir Matthew Baillie Begbie, B.C.'s legendary frontier judge who was "...a terror to all evil doers and a sworn enemy to the use of the knife and revolver."

Richfield on gold-laden Williams Creek in 1868. At left beside the flagpole is the courthouse, very familiar to Judge Begbie. The building stood from 1862 to 1882, then was replaced by a new courthouse which is still in use and preserved as an historic landmark.

Richmond could not control himself and haw-hawed loudly. Barney grabbed the knife, sat down, and passed sentence without batting an eye.

Barney was a real character, founder of Burns Lake and known throughout the Central B.C.-Omineca area where he had, in earlier years, delivered the mail by dog team to many backwoods families. He was well read, and had at one time been asked to consider a political career. He was godfather to my first son born in May 1948, and until his death several years later I enjoyed his informative letters about life in Burns Lake after my transfer from there. There will never be another Barney Mulvaney!

DON'T TELL ME HOW TO RUN MY COURT
by 1st Class Constable J. F. "Jack" French

I was transferred to the North Okanagan community of Enderby during the Depression and have two memories of my courtroom appearances. Working with Constable Jerry Smith was a treat, and he had a great sense of humor as I found out during my first court appearance.

I summonsed a Chinese vegetable peddler, whom I shall refer to as Wong, for running a stop sign, the first case I had after my arrival at the Detachment.

On court day the local Justice of the Peace, Fred Barnes, who was a farmer, made his appearance in his work clothes. He wore bib overalls, a straw hat and smoked a large pipe going full blast. It was a bit of a shock to me as I was used to more conservative deportment on the part of presiding justices.

I opened the hearing in proper form and expected Barnes to read the charge to Wong, but he did not, only asking him what he thought of the circumstances of his arraignment. Confused and unaware of how he should reply, poor Wong said nothing. I noticed Jerry sitting in a corner chuckling to himself as though he expected something of an unusual nature to happen. I soon learned why. When I requested Barnes to read the charge to the accused, I got it good!

He roared at me not to tell him how to run his court, snorting that he had been officiating long before I was born. Then, without further ado, he fined Wong $5 and $1.75 costs and went off to his barn and hay pile.

"The Beak" had given me my first memorable experience in Enderby. The second was when I took the fine to Enderby City Hall. Times were so tough that I was thanked profusely for bringing in much needed revenue.

WHY THE FUSS? WE ONLY KEPT HALF THE FINES
by Corporal P. H. "Spike" Brown

Many years ago, before uniforms were issued, and when practically all the training a policeman received was to be handed a revolver and a badge, a newly recruited Constable was posted to a remote one-man Detachment to replace an officer who had been transferred elsewhere.

Time passed and there came a day when the Superintendent visited him in the course of an inspection tour. While in conversation with the Constable the "brass" asked how he found police work — whether it was to his liking or not.

"First rate," was the reply. "Oh, the salary ain't no hell, but the pickings are good!"

Asked for an explanation, he elaborated: "Well, it's like this. Since the pay is low, the Magistrate put me on to a good thing which helps a lot. Like the last Constable, we split the fine and costs of every second case."

Two Constables found themselves suddenly returned to civilian life, and a new Magistrate was appointed.

Then there was the thoughtful Magistrate who, having fined a speeder $35, suggested he obtain a receipt from the clerk of the court when he paid the fine.

"What do you expect me to do with that?" snapped the disgruntled speeder.

"Save it," replied His Honor. "When you get three of them you get a bicycle."

FROM RURAL JPs TO COUNTY COURT JUDGES
by Assistant Commissioner Cecil Clark

During my 35 years on the Force I got to know personally scores of policemen and heard many of their experiences with "The Beak." Take the memorable occasion in the Cariboo when on a Monday morning Constable E. Bruce Irving placed three blue papers listing charges in front of the local J.P., whom we'll style John Doe. The blue forms identified three morose-looking Saturday night drunks then and there present.

Before the policeman could read the charges, however, His Worship indicated that he had something to say. With a pause in the proceedings, gravely he picked up a blue form from his desk and read out his own name as one of the week-end delinquents. As he finished reading the drunk charge, he asked himself the pertinent question, "How do you plead? Guilty or not guilty?"

For answer he left his seat to range himself beside the other celebrants. Here he uttered one word: "Guilty."

Back again behind his table he scowled down at his interested audience and snapped, "I fine you $10 — and if I catch you before me again I'll make it $20!"

With the same studied gravity he produced from his pocket the necessary $10. Laying it on the table he remarked to the Constable, "Now you can proceed with the rest of the cases."

Then there was Detective-Sergeant Bill MacBrayne's reminiscence of how he once steered a malefactor in front of a Magistrate. The accused, on being asked to plead, said, "Not guilty."

"What d'ye mean, not guilty!" snapped the magistrate. "The policeman brought you here didn't he?"

Which brings to mind Jack Henry's story about Billy Fisher, who at the time was either a County or Supreme Court Judge. Anyway, one evening when Judge Fisher was in Terrace, after dinner he returned to his upstairs room. Opening the French doors he stepped out on to the wooden balcony to view the quiet village scene. Suddenly he noticed, across the road, two characters busily engaged in breaking into the liquor store. He phoned the police and they were rounded up.

When they came before him, one of them attempted an alibi. He said he wasn't there.

"What do you mean you weren't there!" exploded Fisher. "I saw you!"

Not only could the incident be classed as direct evidence but it also resulted in a speedy conviction.

A story told of another Interior Magistrate goes back 50-odd years. He had high hopes of being appointed to a position on a newly formed Game Board, but there was a slip and his prospects didn't jell. Not long after, a policeman brought before him a hunter who pleaded guilty to hunting without a licence.

"I'm not in favor of the enforcement of the Game Act," said the Magistrate by way of revenge, "and I'm dismissing the case."

This curious judgment found its way, on the Constable's report, through all the channels.

At one period in the long and colorful history of the B.C. Provincial Police we had the good fortune to have as Commissioner Colonel John Hugh McMullin. He enlisted in the B.C. Provincial Police as a Constable and eventually rose to command the Force. He was a prime example of those who can "walk with kings and not lose the common touch." In his wide experience of early day B.C. his acquaintances ranged from cowboys to cabinet ministers.

Occasionally, when he drew on this colorful background, some rare anecdotes were produced.

One afternoon apropos of some talk about the Kootenays, he suddenly remarked, "Did you ever hear how the County Court was opened in Greenwood?"

Now as everyone knows, small Interior towns are often very jealous of their standing. The withdrawal of the local policeman was usually the cue for a town meeting, the transfer of the only bank to a more productive community akin to disaster. Conversely, a new court-house is a terrific gain, only equalled if the railway makes the town a divisional point.

So it can be imagined what a boost it was to the town's civic pride when the citizens heard that Greenwood was slated to have a County Court judge. Came finally the great day when the new judge arrived. The next morning he took his seat on the bench to view below him the court registrar, the sheriff, a couple of town lawyers and the local policeman.

Sensitive of the auspicious occasion, the registrar thought it appropriate to voice a few words of welcome, expressing generally the pleasure they felt at the singular honor done to the fair town. It was not a bad speech, and when he had finished the sheriff, with an air of

Greenwood in the early 1900s and, inset, Colonel J. H. McMullin who
headed the Force from 1923-39. Under his leadership it became one of the
most effective in North America.

importance, said he wished to associate himself with all the registrar
had said.

But, strange to say, the Judge didn't seem to be much impressed
by these felicitations. In fact, as he listened his air of boredom verged
on one of impatience. Finally he replied to his well-wishers.

"Mr. Registrar," he said. "While I am sure your sentiments stem
from an honest desire to mark the occasion in fitting style, nevertheless
I must be frank and tell you that, so far as I am concerned, I am
unimpressed.

"Yesterday," he went on, "when I arrived in town no one apparently
had either the good sense or the good manners to meet me at the train,
show me to a hotel, or do any small service that is usually spurred by
genuine hospitality."

As bewilderment clouded the faces of the registrar and the sheriff,
His Honor went on: "Now this lack of consideration, I view in very
strong light. In fact so strongly do I feel on the subject, that I regard
you, Mr. Registrar, and you, Mr. Sheriff, as being both guilty of con-
tempt of court. That being my opinion, I shall fine you each $10!"

It was plain to see the world had crashed around the ears of the
registrar and the sheriff. At His Honor's dictum they could only search
in their pockets for the cash penalty. As they fumbled perhaps they
searched the Judge's unrelenting countenance for some sign of relief.
They saw none. Silent and abashed, they laid the money on their desk.

"Now," said His Honor, as he stepped down from his rostrum and picked up the money from the table, "I think we should all repair across the street and there open the County Court in a more fitting manner!"

There was a pause in Colonel McMullin's story, in keeping with his Irish sense of timing, then he concluded with, "And so they did. Unfortunately toward evening the Judge fell down the stairs and broke his arm."

Then there was the experience of Constable Pat Brabazon. Seems that at Cranbrook many years ago County Court Judge George Thompson was noted for his habit of holding one hand in front of his face as he listened to the evidence, but with one eye peering through a couple of parted fingers. Otherwise, you would have thought he was asleep.

Came a moment in a liquor case when Sergeant George Greenwood described his midnight raid on Mrs. Johnson's resort which happened to be filled with customers. Crown counsel took George through the scene up to his midnight knock at the lady's door.

"Who answered?" asked the prosecutor.

"Mrs. Johnson."

"And what did she say?"

George thought for a moment and replied: "She said, 'Well, Jesus Christ'!"

Old Thompson removed his hand from his face and quietly remarked, "Clearly a case of mistaken identity!"

THREE FEARLESS GOLD-RUSH JUDGES
In southeastern B.C. in 1864 a stampede started to a gold-laden creek the miners called Stud Horse, later sanitized to Wild Horse by sensitive bureaucrats. Some 5-6,000 men, mostly from the United States, flooded the region. Since there was no Magistrate or Constables, the only law was that provided by the miners themselves.

On August 9 a Canadian-Irishman, Thomas Walker, got into an argument with a U.S. miner, "Yeast" Powder Bill, and drew his revolver. Unfortunately for Walker, he merely clipped the end off Yeast Powder's thumb. With his undamaged hand Yeast Powder drew and Walker dropped, a bullet through his heart. "Overland" Bob Evans then started shooting and a free-for-all ensued. Overland Bob was so badly wounded that he was three months recovering, a man named Kelly was stabbed in the back, and Paddy Skie clubbed so hard that he was unconscious for months.

An account of subsequent events was written by D. M. Drumheller in his book, *"Uncle Dan" Drumheller Tells Thrills of Western Trails:*

"A mob was quickly raised by the friends of Tommy Walker for the purpose of hanging Overland Bob and Yeast Powder Bill. Then a law and order organization numbering about 1,000 miners, of which I was a member, assembled. It was the purpose of our organization to order a miners' court and give all concerned a fair trial. Our organization took care of the ... wounded men and put a strong guard around them. The next morning we appointed a lawyer by the name of A. J. Gregory as trial judge and John McClellan sheriff, with authority to appoint as many deputies as he wished. That was the condition of things when Judge Haines (Haynes), the British Columbia Commissioner, rode into camp.

" 'Fifteen hundred men under arms in the queen's dominion. A dastardly usurpation of authority, don't cher know,' remarked Judge Haines. But one little English constable with knee breeches, red cap, cane in his hand, riding a jockey saddle and mounted on a bob-tailed horse, quelled that mob in 15 minutes."

Haynes relieved the "sheriff" of further duties and held an inquest. Although the jury was confused about who shot whom in the gun duel, they felt that Yeast Powder Bill had acted in self defence. A subsequent preliminary hearing agreed and Yeast Powder Bill was set free.

Commissioner John C. Haynes was one of the first to enlist in Police Inspector Chartres Brew's force in 1858. When he arrived at Wild Horse, accompanied by one Constable, he had been 20 days in the saddle from the Okanagan. At the diggings he promptly ordered that all six-guns be left in tent or cabin. The result was dramatic. Afterwards when Colonial Secretary Arthur N. Birch reached Wild Horse after 24 days on horseback from the Fraser River, he reported: "I found the British Columbia mining laws in full force, all customs duties paid, no pistols to be seen and everything as quiet and orderly as it could possibly be in the most civilized district of the colony."

Later, three Constables were stationed at Wild Horse, although there was a temporary shortage when Constable John Carrington left on a trip. It wasn't exactly a pleasure jaunt. By horseback he took a prisoner over 400 miles to Hope, then down the Fraser River to New Westminster. The crime that resulted in a 1,000-mile plus round trip? Murder at least? No. A miner had been charged duty on a ham, was understandably annoyed, raised a fuss and ended in the slammer 500 arduous miles away.

Unfortunately, in April 1867 one of the three Constables at Wild Horse was murdered. He was John Lawson, shot in the head while arresting a horse thief called "One-Ear" Brown.

One-Ear — so named because he had his ear shot off while serving one of his many sentences in a Victoria jail — promptly fled into the U.S. Here he felt safe since police couldn't pursue him across the border. But he overlooked one detail that proved fatal to him. Constable Lawson had been very popular and four miners decided to avenge his death. They also slipped into the U.S. and caught up to One-Ear on a trail. The nervous fugitive had a knife in one hand and a gun in the other. Neither helped. The *British Columbian* newspaper at New Westminster reported the consequence:

"...Three of them raised their guns, double barreled guns, loaded with buckshot and fired simultaneously, literally riddling his dastardly carcass. Returning on the following day, they dug a hole into which they put the remains of Charles Brown, the thief and cowardly murderer. He lies close by the side of the Walla Walla trail, 43 miles south of the boundary line...."

Another Commissioner who served at Wild Horse Creek was Peter O'Reilly, appointed a Stipendiary Magistrate in 1859. At Wild Horse he delivered an address that became a legend, although some historians feel that it should be credited to Commissioner Haynes. However, "Uncle Dan" Drumheller made no reference to it when he described Haynes' arrival at Wild Horse.

By contrast, there is an account in a book with the lengthy title *Sport and Life in the Hunting Grounds of Western America and British Columbia*. It was written by W. A. Baillie-Grohman, a sportsman-developer who arrived in the East Kootenay in 1882. Since there was no stenographer to record O'Reilly's words, there are many variations. According to Baillie-Grohman, when O'Reilly arrived at Wild Horse he addressed a group of miners in front of "the single-roomed cabin which he had turned into a temporary courthouse ... and made a famous speech which is still remembered throughout the mining camps.... Standing near the pole from which floated the Union Jack ... he said: 'Boys, I am here to keep order and to administer the law. Those who don't want law and order can git, but those who stay with the camp, remember on what side of the line the camp is; for, boys, if there is shooting in Kootenay there will be hanging in Kootenay'."

There was no hanging in Kootenay — at least during the gold-rush era — with the only major problem caused by One-Ear Brown. He wasn't a miner, however, but a hood who landed in Victoria in 1858 and was in and out of jail until the four Wild Horse miners permanently closed his file.

The most famous of the frontier judges was Matthew Baillie Begbie. He arrived from England in 1858, an athletic 39-year-old lawyer who could speak fluent French and German, a boxer and tennis player

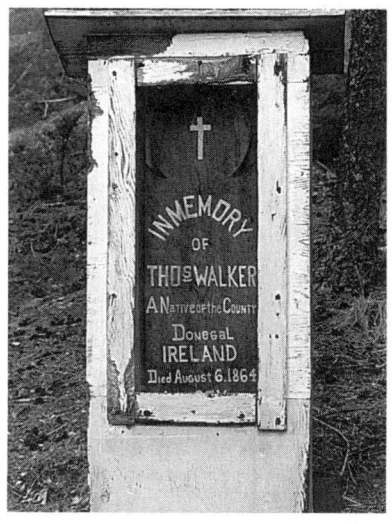

Above: Still standing is the original headboard on Thomas Walker's grave.

Top right: The Dewdney Trail headed eastward some 400 miles from Fort Hope to Wild Horse Creek.

Opposite page: Judge Peter O'Reilly, at left, and Judge J. C. Haynes enforced law and order at Wild Horse Creek in the early 1860s. Both rode horseback to get there, Judge Haynes nearly three weeks in the saddle from the Okanagan.

and a man who loved the outdoors, including hunting and fishing. He was selected because Colonial Secretary Edward Bulwer Lytton wanted a man who "...could, if necessary, truss a murderer up and hang him from the nearest tree."

Begbie was sworn in at Fort Langley on November 19, 1858, when the Colony of British Columbia was established. His athletic build and love of horses and the outdoors soon proved major assets. When gold was discovered in the Cariboo Mountains some 500 miles to the northward of New Westminster in the early 1860s, Begbie regularly held Court in communities which appeared in the new diggings and along the way. Since there was no road to the area until 1863-65, he travelled on horseback or on foot where the treacherous trails became, as he noted: "Utterly impassable for any animal but a man, a goat, or a dog." He was to travel thousands of miles in the saddle, the first years living in a tent and cooking over a fire.

On October 31, 1861, J. T. Scott encountered the Judge in late October in the Cariboo Mountains when winter was in full control. In a letter to the *British Columbian* newspaper at New Westminster he wrote: "On going up the Snow-shoe Mountain I met with Judge Begbie and suite, toiling their way over the snowcapped peaks of Cariboo...."

He always carried his robes and wore them wherever he held court, whether in the open air, a tent, store, saloon or log courthouse. He immediately established a reputation as a no nonsense judge, although with his Van Dyke beard, mustache waxed to sharp points, and imposing size, (nearly six foot six inches) he was formidable without saying a word. Miscreants quickly discovered that he was not only fearless but impartial, with all men equal in his court. This concept was a radical one in an era when native Indians, Chinese and other "foreigners" were considered inferior and treated accordingly.

Writing of him in his "Confidential Report on Officers," Governor James Douglas noted:

"Able, active, energetic and highly talented, Mr. Begbie is a most valuable public servant. I feel greatly indebted to him for the zealous discharge of his official duties and for many services beyond the strict line of official duty. It would be impossible I think to find a person better qualified for the position he fills and for that of Chief Justice when the appointment is made."

As part of the "...many services beyond the strict line of official duty." Begbie just didn't ride around his vast territory. He drew maps, noted geographical features and resources, recorded meteorological data and described the communties. Here is what he wrote about Antler, a gold-rush community which flared briefly. At the time of Begbie's description in 1861 the only access was by trails, all supplies coming over 400 miles on the backs of horses, mules and, the next year, even camels:

"Antler though in itself not well situated either in point of central locality with reference to the other Creeks, or as affording favourable line for Trails in any respect, distance, feed, or hard ground, may be considered as the headquarters of the Cariboo in 1861; there were from 60 to 70 houses in immediate contiguity, many of considerable size and cost and many more scattered up and down the valley; there was a larger population in this Valley probably than in any Town in the colony. There is also a Saw Mill 1½ mile distant; the shops were well furnished: and there were articles of luxury which probably could not be obtained elsewhere beyond New Westminster, e.g. Champagne at $12 per bottle, etc."

News of Begbie's firm but fair judgments travelled widely, being particularly noticed by the lawless element. The consequence was described by the *Victoria Colonist* in its August 17, 1863, edition:

"Everything is very quiet and orderly ... owing in great measure to Mr. O'Reilly's efficiency and the wholesome presence of Judge Begbie who seems to be a terror to evil doers and a sworn enemy to the use of the knife and revolver. Crime in Cariboo has been vigorously checked in its infancy by a firm hand, and seems to have sought some soil more congenial to its growth. The most prejudiced ... on the Creek allows that a security of life and property exists which twelve months ago it would have appeared as useless to expect."

In the early 1860s Dr. Cheadle and Lord Milton made a sightseeing trip across Canada, probably the West's first tourists. They met Judge Begbie near Clinton in 1863. Cheadle later wrote in his book, *Cheadle's Journal:* "Passed Judge Begbie on horseback. Everybody praises his just severity as the salvation of Cariboo and terror of rowdies."

In his "just severity" Begbie spared neither the accused nor the jury if he thought the verdict was wrong. At Williams Lake in 1862 one of his cases involved a man named Gilchrist. In a saloon he and his buddies staged an argument so that Gilchrist could shoot a man named Turner he had a grudge against. The bullet missed Turner, killing an innocent bystander. Gilchrist was charged with murder but the jury found him guilty only of manslaughter. Begbie was appalled.

"Prisoner," he began, in his penetrating voice, "it is far from a pleasant duty for me to have to sentence you only to imprisonment for life.... Your crime was unmitigated, diabolical murder. You deserve to be hanged! Had the jury performed their duty I might now have the painful satisfaction of condemning you to death; and you, gentlemen of the jury, you are a pack of ... horse thieves, and permit me to say, it would give me great pleasure to see you hanged, each and every one of you, for declaring a murderer guilty only of manslaughter."

There are many other instances of Begbie showing displeasure not only with a jury's decision but also with a witness. One clergyman entered the witness box in a somewhat clumsy manner. "Stand up, sir," Begbie admonished the unfortunate man of the cloth. "You look like a sausage skin filled with water."

Of the many stories about him, the most popular one is probably untrue. According to it, on one trip to the Cariboo the Judge was standing on the balcony of the famous Clinton Hotel when he heard below some men plotting revenge because he had sentenced their friend. The Judge listened then calmly returned to his room, got his chamber pot from under the bed and emptied it on them.

Even if the story is untrue, if Begbie had heard such a conversation he wouldn't have been afraid to empty his chamber pot over them. He was not a man intimidated by threats. For instance, writing in the B.C. Provincial Police's official magazine, *The Shoulder Strap*, A. G. Harvey recalled that "On one occasion when the judge and my father were up

The Clinton Hotel in the late 1860s. Legend credits Judge Begbie with emptying his chamber pot from the balcony on some toughs plotting against him.

in the Cariboo, they stopped at a saloon for refreshments. Here they found a professional boxer, just arrived in the country, standing naked to the waist. He was exhibiting his muscles and sinews to the assembled throng and challenging anyone to combat. My father knew of the Judge's ability with the gloves and suggested that he have a 'go' with the man. He declined, however, as he made no claim to professional standing along that line. Just then the boxer turned his back to them and my father touched the burning end of his cigar to it. Wheeling around with a yell, the fellow accused the Judge and dared him to fight. A gleam came into Begbie's eye, off went his coat and out went his fists. In a few minutes the professional had had enough and cheers went up for the winner."

But there were also humorous encounters. Harvey noted that one story involved a Chinaman who had married an Indian woman and applied to the Judge for a divorce. Asked for his grounds, he said he and his wife had to eat out of the same bowl. But since she ate with a big wooden spoon and he with chopsticks, he was being reduced to starvation.

In a mining claim case, where one man pretended to represent two claimholders, Begbie said, "A miner might as well attempt to go to sleep in two bunks." In a case involving boats racing he remarked, "Although it was in evidence that these vessels never race — that is forbidden by the Pilot rules — yet it was ingenuously confessed that they never meet without seeing which of them can go the fastest."

Since Judge Begbie experienced weeks in the saddle, he knew the appalling conditions under which gold-rush Magistrates and policemen had to perform their duties. His letters, preserved at the Provincial Archives, reveal that he was a strong advocate for more policemen and better working conditions. During the Cariboo gold rush in the early 1860s he wrote that "...there was not a magistrate nor a constable to be met within the long ride from Lillooet to the Cariboo — a journey which took a loaded mule train an average of from 28 to 35 days, and which even a light horseman could not expect to accomplish under eight or ten days."

Of the policeman's pay he was very critical, noting that the police were "called upon to perform most thankless duties involving great personal fatigue, exposure and responsibility.... The rates of pay are notoriously insufficient to provide a constable in the Cariboo with more than one meal a day ... without allowing anything for clothes (which I need not remark are extremely expensive and rapidly worn out), tobacco, an occasional stimulant or any of the other extras which a rough mountain life justifies and almost demands...."

Begbie was equally appalled at the accommodation — or lack of it. "At Williams Creek," he wrote, "a log house was built by Mr. Elwyn, which, being divided across the middle, gave accommodation for writing in the one half (a space of about 12 by 16 feet) and on the other half (of equal size, but possessing the inestimable luxury of a fireplace) Mr. Elwyn, his secretary, and three constables, had bunks piled upon each other, in which each man could spread his blankets separately. At

Van Winkle, Mr. O'Reilly had not found the means of providing himself with any such luxury and the whole of the business of the district had to be conducted in a tent, which was the sole protection against the weather for him, and the books and records of the district. The climate in the Cariboo is at times exceedingly wet, as in all high mountainous regions, and it is not unusual to have torrents of rain for a week together almost without intermission. The tent ... I suppose withstands the weather no better than my own, and although it answers very well in tolerable weather or even for a few days of rain and where the camp is changed from time to time, I find that my tent becomes occasionally covered with mildew in the inside, while it is impossible to keep books, etc., dry, and all writing and recording is carried on at the greatest inconvenience. Besides the ground being constantly cold and damp, and there being no opportunity of approaching a fire without going out into the heavy rain, all cooking or drying any articles of apparel becomes extremely irksome. All officers having to remain for any length of time in that district ought to be provided at least with one room having a fireplace where they may at least be sure to meet a dry place to lie on, and the means of warming themselves and drying their clothes, keeping their books, etc., and placing a table so as to be able to write."

In addition to the Cariboo, Judge Begbie held court in other regions of the province, including the remote Cassiar in northwestern B.C. During the gold-rush era he travelled thousands of miles on horseback. One trip alone to Wild Horse Creek involved 800 miles in the saddle. He was to serve for 36 years, the last 23 years as Chief Justice of the Province. In 1875 in recognition of his service he was knighted by Queen Victoria.

He remained active until his death at 75 on June 11, 1894, from stomach cancer. In his will he requested that his funeral be simple, with no wreaths or flowers. Instead Premier T. Davie ordered a state funeral in honor of his achievements. It was one of the largest, if not the largest, ever held in Victoria. Included were detachments of soldiers, community service groups, two bands and the Fire Brigade, the hearse drawn by six horses. Thousands of citizens lined the funeral route in a silent farewell.

He was buried at Ross Bay Cemetery, among many of the province's pioneers. Despite his request for no flowers, they were present in abundance.

Of all the tributes to him, the one he probably would have appreciated most was by a miner. It was brief and sincere: "Begbie was the biggest man, the smartest man, the best looking man, and the damndest man that ever came over the Cariboo road."

Cut firewood, sweep the floor, bake bread, do the laundry, order supplies for six months of isolation and, oh yes, police an area nearly as large as England. It was all part of being a bachelor in a

ONE-MAN DETACHMENT IN CASSIAR COUNTRY

by Corporal R. J. "Jack" Meek

"...and don't forget, Meek. Fly the flag!" Those were the parting words of Thomas W. S. Parsons, the Deputy Commissioner, B.C. Provincial Police, as the launch bearing him pulled away from the shore at McDames Creek in July, 1935.

"Yes, sir," I responded, not quite getting his point. But in the next several months when the Detachment was becoming a working part of the police machine, I came to understand. In the meantime, I had to familiarize myself with my patrol area which I learned was almost the size of England — and all mountains.

The Cassiar country of Northwestern B.C. was wilderness except for a couple of trading posts on Dease Lake and 75 miles of "road" between Telegraph Creek and Dease Lake. Actually, the road was little more than the trail which Captain Moore and his sons had slashed out in 1873. It wasn't unusual for the few users to spend a day or more just getting out of one mudhole. In summer the Dease River and Lake were the main travel route, with Lower Post some 215 miles downstream from the lakehead. In winter dogs and snowshoes became the means

Opposite page: The Detachment office-residence at McDames Creek. The author built it for $20 — the cost of the two front windows. Victoria Headquarters, however, refused to reimburse him for the outlay, considering the windows an unnecessary frill.

The police dog team on mountain-flanked Dease Lake. So isolated was McDames Creek in winter that the author had to make a 500-mile return trip by dog team to Telegraph Creek for mail.

of travel. In future years I would make many lonely one-man dog team trips to Lower Post, a return trek of nearly 300 miles.

The white man's history dated back to the early 1870s when two prospectors named McCullough and Thibert discovered gold near Dease Lake. A rush started and among those attracted were B.C. frontiersman Captain W. Moore and his three sons. So remote was Dease Lake that they were 62 days fighting their way from Wrangell at the mouth of the Stikine River. In 1874 a strike was made at Mc-Dames Creek and that summer there were some 5,000 men in the area. The gold rush, however, was short lived and the land reverted to the Indians and a few trappers and prospectors. When I arrived there were only nine white men in the area.

The isolation took some getting used to. The final boat to the "outside" chugged upstream about the middle of September, taking with it my last reports and returns to Telegraph Creek, from where they went to Division Headquarters at Prince Rupert. The first boat in summer arrived after the ice went out on Dease Lake, sometime around the second week in June. We craved, after being cut off from commercial sources of supply all the long winter, for fresh fruit, vegetables, bakery items and, of course, mail. In winter if I wanted to get my mail and see the "bright lights" it meant a 500-mile, 20-day round trip by dog team to Telegraph Creek which contained some 200 people in a community built almost entirely of logs.

One memorable winter McDames Creek ran out of yeast, and due to an extreme cold snap we had no sourdough. This calamity meant no bread, among other things. The Hudson's Bay store had nothing to offer, so the whole community was without yeast. Fortunately, old Joe Sexsmith had lived most of his life above the 60th parallel and he knew that yeast is in the air throughout the North. It took him about a week to capture the right yeast plant which he carefully cultivated. Within two weeks all of us had our sourdough pots busily working until we acquired fresh yeast next June on the first boat.

My first winter, however, passed more or less routinely, although Deputy Commissioner's parting words, "...and don't forget, Meek. Fly the Flag!" were not forgotten. As a consequence, when summer came in 1936 I planned to put his words into effect. I would have an impressive show for the July 1 Dominion Day celebrations. A pole had been erected and I was resplendent in full dress uniform on the morning of "the day" when we hoisted the flag. Many Indians came into the post, as well as all the nine white men in the area. To mark the day, I thought some sort of celebration should take place, and what was better than a sports meet?

For the McDAMES CREEK FIRST ANNUAL DOMINION DAY SPORTS I drew up a schedule of events I thought appropriate. There was a good number of Indian children, and I anticipated I'd get some exciting contests involving the young men, considering their fine physical condition. Some of the older white men acted as judges and starters. The first few races were for the young ones but they didn't go over very well. The children didn't seem to like the idea and some of the smaller ones began to cry as they were not used to all the attention they received.

The first big race was for ladies. After a lot of urging I finally encouraged some half dozen youthful squaws to the starting line. But they were full of giggles and blushes and kept wandering off to talk to their friends or engage in other interests. At last all was ready. "One, two, three...GO!" I shouted when, for an instant, I had them all at the starting mark.

Several drifted in the general direction of the finishing line, but the others simply meandered about. I then realized that they had never been in a race, had never seen one, didn't know what was expected of them and, therefore, had no competitive spirit. So, nobody won. Conversely, in keeping with Indian philosophy, nobody lost.

My only problem was prizes since I had never considered the possibility of everyone being a winner. But one way or another I managed to furnish prizes to each of the participants. We finished with the traditional Indian gambling game played with sticks, called "lahal" in those parts. The Indians won everything from the white men, which somehow or other seemed to even things up.

The First Annual Dominion Day Sports had given me my first exposure to the Indian character. Soon I was to receive additional education in what could be termed a "Prison without Bars."

As every policeman knows, you have to temper blind justice with a pinch of common horse-sense. I was just as guilty as most of the other law-enforcement officers in overlooking petty infractions. We didn't have a lockup at McDames so I didn't go looking for customers. Once, however, at Lower Post on the complaint of a priest, I had to prosecute a young Indian named Tom. He was sentenced to 30 days in jail, so I had to get him the 140 miles or so back up the Dease River to the Detachment. I had to use all my ingenuity to keep him under custody since there was no lockup at Lower Post either. I gave him a stern warning that if I allowed him to spend the night with his parents he had to be at the boat early next morning or I'd leave without him (!!). I hadn't the foggiest idea of what I'd do if he didn't show up. Fortunately, Tom, in turn, hadn't any idea of what he would be up against if he wasn't there.

He did appear as ordered, and when I got him to the Detachment I had him cut wood, feed the dogs, and do other chores. I had to cook for him, something he seemed to relish. Not because of my culinary skill but because it was "store food," apart from the bread which I baked.

He slept in a tent outside the barracks where, from time to time, the local Indians would saunter over to the Detachment to talk with my "prisoner." I didn't mind as I had kept his rifle and knew he wouldn't take off without it. But still he was supposed to be serving time and I was a bit nervous about him staying without bounds, especially when one or two of the young native women started fluttering their eyelids. So, with a great show of craftiness mixed with a little black magic, I drew a line on the ground to designate

The log community of Telegraph Creek and Thomas Parsons when he had been promoted to Commissioner (Commander) of the Force.

the confines of his "jail." I told Tom it was the boundary beyond which he must not dare to go. My mumbo-jumbo worked. He would carefully edge up to the line until his moccasined toes just touched it, but he wouldn't cross over.

When his time was up I let him go, but there he was in the bush over a hundred miles from his home. I paid his fare on a launch that passed by. But neither the B.C. Provincial Police nor Indian Affairs would repay me. "Not their policy" was the bureaucratic excuse.

After Tom left I was back to cooking for myself, although that didn't mean the "bacon and beans" grub of prospecting legend. Even when there was no supply boat for six months we had variety in our daily fare. Indeed, a great deal of ingenuity and skill went into producing diversified meals. Cooking on the trail, especially, was a challenge. The finest trail cooking I experienced was on a winter dog-team trip.

At McDames Creek Detachment we often travelled with others, especially in winter. It was safer for one thing, and in that lonely country a bit of companionship was always welcome. As I had a reputation of being a bit fussy because I washed my hands more than once a day, I was usually elected camp cook — something of a "con" job because whoever was cook carried on until somebody complained, then he became cook. But I didn't mind since the others had to make camp, cut firewood, and feed the dogs.

In the late winter of 1938 a friend and I travelled by dog team to "downtown" Telegraph Creek, as already noted a return journey of

Indian trappers from Telegraph Creek in March. They had the luxury of a tent and stove. On his lonely one-man patrols that could last for several weeks, the author had only a canvas fly for shelter, even in blizzards and temperature -40° F and colder.

some 500 miles. Between Dease Lake and Telegraph Creek a herd of several hundred caribou passed close to us, their hoofs giving out a curious clicking sound as they bounced along. As we needed some fresh meat, I shot one.

Quickly we butchered the animal, fed some to the dogs, kept a bit for ourselves, and tied the rest up on a tall pine tree for our return journey. It had taken less than an hour. Then on to the bright lights of the only hamlet in the Detachment.

My business finished, I made plans to return. Two or three men wanted to come along as they had various errands and jobs to do. One of them was called Blackie, although I never did know his real name. He was dark, balding, fiftyish, with quick sure movements that indicated economy of effort and complete confidence in himself. He had the reputation of being the best trail cook in the Cassiar. I tried to learn all I could from him. He claimed he used very few spices: salt and pepper, of course, a few bay leaves, a garlic or two — and that was about it.

Five dog teams pulled out of Telegraph Creek early one March morning, and by evening we drew up at our little meat cache. While the other three made camp I gave all my attention to Blackie.

I watched in admiration — almost fascination — as Blackie neatly cut the caribou haunch into steaks. Then he added a pinch of salt here, a rub of garlic there, a whisk of pepper, and all the other little touches which mark the difference between a chef and ordinary men. Blackie always packed a large round iron skillet, and on this the sizzling steaks gave forth a tantalizing aroma. I can't remember what accompanied the meat but, it too, received a touch of his genius. I made the tea and bannock. Then, as the cold northern sun set and the snowclad mountains gleamed pink and gold, Blackie announced, with all the dignity of a State Ball, that supper was ready. I cut into the succulent caribou steak. Then I took my first bite.

Did Blackie come up to expectations? Was he the gourmet chef he was reputed to be? Could it really be that good?

It was!

On most patrols, however, I travelled alone and that northern staple, bannock, was standard fare. The main reason for its popularity is simplicity, being a mixture of flour, salt, baking powder and water. Seasoned northerners mix it right in the flour sack, toss it into the frying pan, make a little hole in the center to aid cooking, then prop it in front of a pine or spruce fire. While bannock is certainly very plain, the invigorating air — down to -30° F and colder — camp atmosphere and a hard day's travel bestowed a hearty appetite.

With the gaining of more experience I took less and less with me when on patrol — whether by boat, sleigh, horse or on foot. The canvas covering for a sleigh was a windbreak at night, a tent was too heavy and cumbersome. Food became simple, as I found I could get along quite comfortably on straight meat when on the trail. I once experimented by eating nothing but meat and fish for about two months. I felt in excellent shape and, as a bonus, the combination had the effect of inducing very healthy gums.

Feeding the sleigh dogs was a daily chore. Police dogs received a ration of one pound of corn-meal or rice, and one pound of cracklings a day. (Cracklings are dried chips of pork which were cooked along with the other food.) To carry all the dog food needed on a long patrol was an impossibility, so we erected caches for both dogs and ourselves. The Indians were told that it was "government grub," but if they were out of food they could use what they needed. In my several years at the Detachment this privilege was never abused and an Indian who took something from the cache invariably told me and usually brought me a fish or bit of moose meat during the summer months as payment. Cooking dog food on the trail was a bit awkward and for most patrols we found that sleigh dogs worked best if they were fed meat or fish.

Summer travel was less of a challenge to feed the dogs. They were usually tied up to their kennels but I tried to take them for a bit of a run every day or two. Most of the dogs had a small backpack and could carry 10 to 20 pounds, sufficient food for a week of bush travel. Usually we could supplement this supply by dividing a rabbit or two which we caught in wire snares set out each evening.

One experience I had with dogs and their food didn't involve me directly but it did leave a lasting memory. It involved some Indian huskies which, with some exceptions, in summer are fed little — if anything. As a consequence, they are on a perpetual hunt for food of any kind, as the following incident demonstrates.

In the spring of 1938 I received instructions to proceed to Lower Post to keep order for a few weeks. Trappers in the vast hinterland of the Cassiar usually had the choice of two, three, or four trading posts at which to dispose of their furs and shop for supplies, and seemed to favor one in particular each year. Perhaps word got around by "moccasin telegraph" that the majority intended to gather at one of the locations. In 1938 Lower Post was the most popular, hence my orders to be there. The Hudson's Bay Company's trader was a young Scot named Jimmy Buchan, a very fine chap who, I believe, was later killed while serving with the Royal Canadian Air Force in World War Two. He had a good sense of humor, and he and I got along very well together. He had a young dog named Rover, big and slobbery, and always hungry. He had no reason to be since he was fed regularly, unlike the Indian dogs.

One June morning, a typical Lower Post summer day with half a dozen dogs sniffing here and there for scraps from garbage or other sources, Jimmy started making bread. He mixed up a large batch of dough while I watched with considerable interest, always being keen to pick up hints useful in food preparation. When he had kneaded the dough he placed it in the warm sun to rise, covering it with a dish towel. I thought the protection was rather skimpy, but as he had more experience than I in making bread, I conceded that he knew what he was about. We both had other duties which kept us busy for about an hour. Then he approached me with a perplexed look and asked what I had done with the dough. Since I had not concerned myself with it in any way, I was puzzled by what he meant until he explained that the mix had vanished.

Then we saw a strange sight. Jimmy's dog was wandering aimlessly about, obviously much bloated and in pain, followed by five or six of the Indians' canines. We knew at once that we had found the culprit responsible for the disappearance of the equivalent of six loaves of rising dough. So did the dogs trailing the suffering animal. Every three or four minutes the dough being warmed in Rover's belly would expand, and as it had to escape there was only one way for it to go — the back way. Poor Rover would eliminate a bun or two which his admiring friends immediately gobbled up. He was the goose laying the golden eggs, the most popular dog in Lower Post — if not to Jimmy certainly to the hungry Indian dogs. It was the funniest circumstance I have ever witnessed. As the stomach pains of the thief increased, his four-legged pals would start wagging their tails in anticipation. Then when he had provided the latest bakery confection, dispose of it in a flurry of fur and teeth, all trying desperately to get their share. Rover's ordeal lasted for two hours. But for several days he had a retinue of dogs following him, hoping for a repeat performance.

In the Cassiar, treatment of dogs ranged from cruel to considerate. One experience I had, however, made me think that being considerate is a somewhat relative term. But under the circumstances, it probably was the kindest treatment.

Sometime around the middle of July 1936 when I was stationed at McDames Creek, I was informed by Indians that Old Jim Wheeler was dead. They were quite sure he had shot himself. Jim lived alone near the confluence of French Creek where it joins the Dease, about 40 miles downstream from McDames.

In the remote parts of the province a coroner's jury consisted of six men, and that was about all I could muster in that lonely land. We piled into the police launch which Indians called *Dechua*, meaning "porcupine" because it swam so low in the water.

On the trip down I heard men talking about Old Wheeler. Years ago he had left a secure job in Wrangell, Alaska, and headed up into the Dease River country to prospect for gold. He had been attracted by an intriguing story of a very rich pocket of lode somewhere on the headwaters of French Creek. The key to finding it was a square and compasses carved on a large granite boulder on top of a hill. Evidently the discoverer was a Freemason. Whoever he was, the original prospector wrote out the whereabouts in "a little red pocketbook."

At Wheeler's place, everything pointed to suicide. His cabin was orderly, he'd shot his dogs then he'd shot himself with his rifle. Although the body was pretty far gone by the time we got there, the coroner and his jury did their job. Then we dug a grave, and I read the funeral service. I wondered how many hundreds of prospectors and trappers, men who opened up this country in the early days, ended up in abject poverty, or took their lives when they came to the End of The Trail.

I was fascinated by the will-o'-the-wisp that had dominated the life of Jim Wheeler. I discovered over the next few years that a number of others had been involved in the story one way or another.

As far as I could piece together, a prospector many years ago discovered a mother lode on French Creek. He carved a square and compasses as his reference point, then left for Wrangell. He got to Telegraph Creek and set off down the Stikine River, but never arrived at Wrangell. I never learned his real name. He was simply identified as "The Freemason."

Later, someone turned up at Wrangell with the French Creek gold and the little red pocketbook. Rumor had it that the little red pocketbook surfaced in San Francisco, which may have been the source of Jim Wheeler's obsession. It seems fairly certain that the discoverer of the lode and who owned the little red pocketbook was murdered on his way down the Stikine to Wrangell, although I could never find any reference to a murder in our police files.

The story was strong enough to induce several people in Teslin in the early 1930s to fly into the headwaters of French Creek. As one of my informants wrote, "...looking for a granite boulder on top of a sheep range somewhere near Wolf Lake. They crashed and were either killed or died later." Because all of this was in Yukon territory it didn't affect the B.C. Provincial Police.

Piecing together all the many scattered accounts collected over about 10 years, it seems that at least six people died (including Old

Wheeler) looking for that mysterious symbol on a granite stone at the head of an obscure stream slightly north of the B.C.-Yukon border. Pretty elusive, but it made wonderful story-telling around campfires in Northern Detachments.

At the Detachment itself, life was never dull, despite the isolation. By morse code I made daily contact with Prince George and other stations. Then there was a fair amount of office work such as keeping the Police Diary, month-end reports, status of rations and dog feed, payment of wolf bounty, fur pelt returns and other uniquely northern memoranda. Then in 1939, after five years in the Cassiar, I was transferred to Vancouver. In those five years there had been quite a change in the "outside" world.

For instance, when I took over McDames Detachment it had taken me three weeks to reach the post from Vancouver. I made the return journey in "only" five days, travelling 650 miles by plane, 787 by train, and 110 by car, 1,547 miles to get from one Detachment in B.C. to another. After leaving the ice and snow of McDames Creek, Vancouver was fresh and lush, with crocus pushing up and robins on green lawns.

Then onto *Police Motor Launch 14*, flagship of the Police's Marine Section. (See front cover.) We patrolled the "Graveyard of the Pacific" — the western, or outside, coast of Vancouver Island. As a relief radio operator I spent most of the summers travelling from one Divison Headquarters to another — including a couple of weeks as fingerprint operator at Oakalla Prison.

With the outbreak of World War Two police forces across the country were declared a protected occupation. Nevertheless, quite a large percentage of B.C. Policemen purchased their discharge and entered the Armed Forces. I left at the end of 1941, and joined the RCAF.

After almost two years training on how to navigate and drop a bomb, I was posted to 626 Squadron at Wickenby, England, as a navigator on Lancasters of No. 1 Group. Took part in the Battle of Berlin, devastating Happy Valley (the Ruhr), and finished up with D Day activities — my 30th operation being a low-level daylight attack on Caen. I was fortunate in being able to walk away from a couple of crash landings — and most fortunate indeed in being awarded the Distinguished Flying Cross, and — rarest of all — the Conspicuous Gallantry medal.

When hostilities ended, getting back to civilian life was a conundrum. However, I had had such good rapport with Indians in northern B.C. I felt I could contribute to their welfare as an Indian Agent. So I received an appointment as Agent for the Yukon, where I spent the next 10 years. I felt comfortable dealing with my Indian friends and enjoyed the outdoor life.

I even heard a few more obscure references to Jim Wheeler and the Mason's Little Red Pocket Book. But when I left the Yukon at the close of 1955, the boulder with its carved square and compasses remained the concealed enigma it had been since it was carved many years ago.

Highway patrol van in the early 1940s. It was replaced by the coupe, bottom right, which proved more satisfactory.

"OFFICER, IT HAPPENED THIS WAY!"

The following are excerpts from written statements submitted to police on accident report forms. The drivers were instructed to give a brief account of the accident in their own words. The sex of the driver is bracketed following the statement.

Coming home, I drove into the wrong house and collided with a tree I don't have. (F)

I thought my window was down, but I found it was up when I put my hand through it. (M)

I collided with a stationary truck coming the other way. (F)

A truck backed through my windshield into my wife's face. (M)

The guy was all over the road. I had to swerve a number of times before I hit him. (F)

I pulled away from the side of the road, glanced at my mother-in-law, and headed for the embankment. (M)

The gentleman behind me struck me on the backside and then went to rest in the bush with just his rear end showing. (F)

In an attempt to kill a fly, I drove into a telephone pole. (M)

I thought I could squeeze between two trucks when my car became squashed. (F)

I had been shopping for a few plants all day and was on my way home. As I reached an intersection a hedge sprang up obscuring my vision. I did not see the other car. (F)

I had been driving my car for 40 years when I fell asleep at the wheel and had the accident. (M)

The accident occurred when I was attempting to bring my car out of a skid by steering it into the other vehicle. (M)

The other car attempted to cut in front of me, so I, with my right bumper, removed his left tail light. (M)

To avoid hitting the car in front I struck the pedestrian. (F)

I told the police I was not injured, but on removing my hat I found I had a fractured skull. (M)

My car was legally parked as it backed into the other vehicle. (M)

I had been learning to drive with power steering. I turned the wheel to what I thought was enough and found myself in a different direction going the opposite way. (F)

I was backing my car out of the driveway in the usual manner when it was struck by the other car in the same place it had been struck several times. (M)

I was on the way to the doctor with rear end trouble when my universal joint gave way, causing me to have an accident. (M)

I was taking my canary to the hospital. It got loose in the car and flew out the window. The next thing I saw was his rear end and there was a crash. (M)

As I approached the intersection, a stop sign suddenly appeared in a place where no stop sign had ever appeared before. I was unable to stop in time to avoid the accident. (M)

An invisible car came out of nowhere, struck my car and vanished. (M)

I was sure the old fellow would never make it to the other side of the road when I struck him. (F)

When I saw I could not avoid the collision, I stepped on the gas and crashed into the other car. (M)

The pedestrian had no idea which direction to go, so I ran over him. (F)

Atlin in June 1900.

130 POUNDS OF FIGHTING?? POLICEMAN

Unbeknownst to the author, the one-armed man whose Luger he carefully examined was a hunted murderer.

by Special Constable Guy Lawrence

It was 1902 and I had been hired as a Special Constable at the Atlin Detachment in far northwestern B.C. One evening Mr. Graham, the Gold Commissioner who had been a member of the Provincial Police for 17 years prior to being promoted to Mining Recorder and then Gold Commissioner, came into the police office and asked if any of the other men were around.

When finding they were not, he said, "Word has just come up from down town that Paddy is causing a disturbance, I guess you will have to go down and pick him up and bring him in. He is not a dangerous character but you better take a billy along. Don't lose your head, and for God's sake don't go calling on everybody for assistance — if the Mounties have a name to keep up — so have we."

I was 19 at the time, weighing somewhere between 125 and 130 pounds. This was my first assignment on town duty, and having seen Paddy a few times I guessed I might have my hands full. Paddy was really a Scotsman, and when sober was not a bad fellow. We had

Blackwater Telegraph Station where the author examined the murderer's Luger —
then gave it back to him.

Top: Atlin Detachment in 1898. The man in the striped coat is Gold
Commissioner Graham.

previously had a few chats together and I found out that he had once
been in the 42nd Black Watch. After serving seven years with the colors
he had seemingly drifted. He was now a recent arrival from Dawson
in the Yukon where he had taken part in some middleweight bouts
without much success. The Mounties had finally run him out of Yukon
Territory because he was more or less a vagrant.

I found him on Pearl Street with quite a crowd gathered around
him. He was very busy yelling out that he was willing to take on all
comers; but he was almost too drunk to stand up straight. As he
weighed at least 35 pounds heavier than myself, I think the crowd
thought there was going to be some fun. As I got close to him, suddenly
an inspiration struck me, and I shouted in stentorian tones: "All right,
fall in the Black Watch — party shun — left turn, quick march." Like
an old war horse he snapped to attention, and side by side we marched
up to the jail.

When opposite the door I gave one more command and said, "Party right wheel," and through the door we went. One of the other Constables had in the meantime returned, and together we searched Paddy, then locked him up.

Next morning he asked me how he got there, and holding out a dollar bill he begged me to go down town and bring him up a bracer. He had hidden the money in his sock.

The following day it was my duty to buy a steamboat ticket for him and escort him across the lake on the old sternwheeler *Scotia*. When we reached the portage on the other side of the lake I handed Paddy $5 which had been given me by Mr. Graham to turn over to him with instructions that he keep going.

Five days later Paddy was back. This time he did not linger in the town of Atlin but headed for the mining town of Discovery, seven miles distant. He kept out of the way of police, but there were others who noted that whilst they never saw him take a drink yet he always seemed well lit up.

For quite a while this mystery was never solved. Then one morning a saloon keeper went into his back storage room where he kept small barrels of whisky. He found Paddy seated beside a barrel quietly reading a periodical. Promptly the saloon keeper ordered him out, and doubtless Paddy was quite willing to go. But he found this rather difficult with the saloon keeper eyeing him because he was attached to the barrel of whisky by a small rubber hose which was connected, one end to the bung of the barrel, and the other end to a small flask in his hip pocket. Paddy got 14 days this time, after which we never saw him again and concluded he had given up "mining" in Atlin and left the district for good.

(In 1902 Special Constable Lawrence was involved in an incident which could have involved an armed battle. But order was maintained by a few B.C. Provincial Policemen and a government official who were determined that justice, not mob law, would prevail.)

Early April 1902 found the placer mining camp of Atlin in a great stir.

At that time most of the placer diggings were worked by individual miners, the majority of whom owned their own properties, or leased them from some absent owner. There were, however, four or five large companies who worked groups of claims by hydraulicing. Some of these companies would use three monitors and employ quite a number of men, working two, 12-hour shifts.

One of these companies decided to bring in Oriental labor to work their large property, and do away with the white labor entirely except perhaps for a foreman. The manager of the company did not make his decision in a hurry, nor did he make a secret of it, and word traveled around the camp of what he meditated doing. All miners, both owners of claims and any men they happened to be employing, were deeply incensed. They were determined that the Atlin mining camp was not going to be used as a base for cheap labor.

At that time Commissioner Graham was away on vacation. Ned

Thaine, his senior clerk, was in charge. There were three Provincial Police in the camp and me, whose duty it was to work in the court room and guard prisoners.

The Chief of that small Detachment was Walter Owen, who in later years became Chief Warden at Oakalla Prison. The second Constable was William Vickers, known to all as "Billy" Vickers. He later became Chief of Police in Prince Rupert for a number of years. The third Constable was Harry Heal.

The company manager of this hydraulic company carried through his threat and some 38 Japanese miners arrived over the ice on the lake in two large horse sleighs. Each of these Orientals carried a .44 rifle with him, but whether the rifles were loaded or just intended as a bluff I cannot say.

The white men immediately dropped their tools and headed for the town of Atlin where they held an "indignation meeting." Many of these men had come in from creeks far distant. They all were very determined, but were quite orderly.

The mining company lost no time and after having rested the Orientals an hour in Atlin they hustled them to their property which was on McKee Creek, 13 miles down the lake. The white men now appealed to Mr. Thaine, but he decided to take no action against the influx of Oriental labor.

The next morning the white men decided to walk down the lake and bring the Japanese out and ship them back to where they had come from. Though still quite orderly there was every evidence that the slightest spark might cause serious bloodshed as these Japanese were armed.

About 10 a.m., 300 miners walked through the town and down on to the lake. Mr. Thaine, anticipating this move, instructed me to arm myself with the regular service revolver and come down to the lake with him. He held in his hand a copy of the Riot Act.

Going out on the lake a little distance and where the winter trail turned south for McKee Creek he stood beside the trail and, bidding me stand beside him, waited for the white men to pass.

The trail was good but very narrow and on each side was deep snow. Soon the miners came along. None of the 300 was armed, and not one carried so much as a stick. On account of the trail being so narrow the men had to walk in single file. Quite naturally this made a long file of men.

As soon as the first man came along Mr. Thaine started to read the Act. Every passing man had grim determination written on his face; none spoke to us, none jeered. They just continued on their journey down the lake.

Mr. Thaine and I returned to the office, and a consultation was held between him and Constable Walter Owen. They decided that Owen and Vickers would take a dog team and make straight for the company property. Here they could make every effort to see that a peaceful settlement to the whole trouble could be made.

When the two Constables arrived they found that the Japanese, still armed, had been installed in a large log cabin. The white miners in very deep snow were scattered around sitting or standing in groups alongside small campfires — but not on company property.

A meeting was held as soon as possible between the company manager, a delegation of three of the miners, the two policemen, and the Japanese overseer. The outcome of the meeting was that the Orientals would immediately leave the camp. It was by now quite dark, and it was decided that the management would start the foreign laborers out next day. The white miners sat around their campfires all that night. They were determined to accept no promises for the deed.

Next day the Japanese started back, still with their rifles, and the incident was closed. Great credit is due both Constable Owen and Constable Vickers for the tactful way they tackled a difficult problem which might easily have caused great bloodshed.

(Guy Lawrence was to spend almost his entire life in Northern B.C. as a telegraph operator on the Yukon Telegraph Line which connected Vancouver with Dawson City in the Yukon some 1,900 miles to the northward. While at Blackwater Station between Quesnel and what is today Prince George, he unknowingly had an encounter with Charley Benton, a halfbreed from the Fraser Valley who had murdered two U.S. lawmen and who was the object of an intense search. (See page 97.)

(One day Benton turned up at Bobtail Lake Telegraph Station, the one above Lawrence's, riding a horse and leading another. The operator, Dick Smith, was feeling downcast since his horse had died that morning after eating loco weed. Benton, however, was willing to sell his spare and they made a deal. But Benton refused to give Smith a bill of sale. For Benton, the consequence was disastrous. Smith now paid close attention to him and suddenly realized, to his horror, that the man answered the description of a murderer recently sent over the telegraph line. But Benton left without incident and Smith quickly telegraphed Quesnel:

("The murderer ... whose description was sent over the wire three weeks ago has just passed by here heading for Quesnel, where he should reach tomorrow night. He has a steel right hand covered with a glove, is armed with a heavy Luger pistol, better advise police at once. He is riding a sorrel horse branded on the right shoulder, and carries one small roll of blankets and one gunny sack tied on the back of his saddle."

(When the Quesnel operator notifed Smith that the police had been informed, he also requested that Smith send no further remarks about Benton over the wire. For this reason, Lawrence was unaware that the murderer of two U.S. lawmen was heading his way. He was soon to find out.)

About 11 a.m. the next morning, I was casting for trout when I saw a lone horseman riding towards the bridge. I immediately ceased fishing so that I could pass the time of day with him.

Horse and man came toward me slowly, and when the man came abreast he eased himself in the saddle and pulled his horse up. Then carefully looking me over he asked how far it was to Quesnel, and seemed surprised it was 44 miles and quite a day and a half ride to where the ferry operated. The man now seemed in no hurry. He dismounted, and stretched himself, saying that he was quite saddle sore. "Is this a good stream for fish," he said , "I could do with a mess of trout, am fed up with my trail fare as I have seen no signs of game all the way down."

"Oh, yes," I replied, "the Blackwater River is notorious for rainbow trout; here take these two, I have more than I need and can easily catch some more." The man eagerly accepted the trout and started to open up the gunny bag to put them in.

I now noted the Luger pistol attached to the man's belt. Firearms interested me and without hesitation I asked the man if I could take a look at it. The man gave me a searching look, then calmly handed over the gun. After hefting the gun for a while and pointing it upstream, I handed it back to the man, exclaiming, "That is a finely balanced weapon, one does not see many of them on the trail, in fact that is the first one I have seen in this district." The man took the weapon in his left hand and returned it to the holster, and said nothing. Soon the man left, and as he had a two-mile hill to climb, he walked his horse.

I now went on with my fishing, and having caught another good sized trout, closed up my Bristol steel rod and returned to the station.

That night the man camped just south of Swan Lake, where an Austrian had a small ranch and also served meals to travelers on the trail to those who wished.

The next day was very hot, and the man headed south had made such good time that by noon he found himself on the west side of the Fraser River, and could see the small town of Quesnel across the river. He decided to take a long rest and cross the river on the last ferry for that day. Close beside him was a fenced meadow. Removing the bars from the one entrance, he led his horse into the lush grass, removed the saddle, and placed hobbles on the animal. Then choosing a shaded spot where he could command a view of the entrance to the field he lay down. Eventually he must have fallen into a sound sleep.

Here he was captured by Constable Anderson and his men, returned to Washington and sentenced to life imprisonment. Dick Smith was highly complimented for his recognition of the wanted man from the description sent out.

I didn't know quite what to think, other than I had held that man's gun, the only one the man carried, and that the man had voluntarily handed it to me. It was evident that the man did not think me very bright. I hate to admit it, but I keenly examined the gun — but not the owner.

Dick Smith was later transferred to Prince George where for some years he was the telegraph agent, becoming well known to thousands of residents and travellers. Guy Lawrence at 85 wrote a very interesting book on his experiences, Forty Years on the Yukon Telegraph.

Atlin in winter, the frozen lake
in the foreground.

Summer patrol on Atlin Lake with the
ancient 10-horse Johnson outboard.

The White Pass and Yukon
locomotive which served the
world's shortest railway and which
Vic Stevens looked after
during the winter.

THE COOL CROSSING

Atlin Lake in northwestern B.C. is the province's
largest natural waterway. The inexperienced policeman
learned that crossing it in a December blow is
memorable — and dangerous.

by 1st-Class Constable T. J. L. "Tom" Kelly

I arrived in Atlin in mid-September 1941 to take over the one-man
Detachment from Charlie Bennett. My wife and I were married in
Prince Rupert on September 11. We left for Atlin the same day, travel-
ling via CPR boat to Skagway, Alaska, then by the White Pass & Yukon
Railway to Carcross, Y.T., and from there by a small bush plane to our
destination. It was a unique honeymoon as we were accompanied by
Inspector Ernie Gammon who had decided it was a good time to
inspect the Detachment.

Still a 3rd Class Constable, and a city raised kid from Vancouver,
I was completely inexperienced with most facts of life in an isolated,
frontier type place like Atlin. Bea, my wife of four days, was no better
off, having lived all her life in Prince Rupert. However, we soon got
used to gas lamps, outside toilets, and water delivered from the lake
at 10 cents a bucket. I inherited a dog team that Charlie Bennett had
put together, and a 16-foot clinker-built rowboat with a rather ancient
10 h.p. Johnson outboard motor for patrols of the various waterways.
The motor was the kind that one started by wrapping a length of rope
around the top of the flywheel and pulling like hell. Being utterly
ignorant of such contraptions and too proud to admit it, I cranked
myself by rope about halfway across the lake the first time I attempted
to start it up. When it finally did catch at full throttle, I almost lost boat,
motor, and my life, as it nearly threw me over the side.

By early December, Bea and I were quite settled in, and already in
debt for a huge winter's supply of food, ordered from Vancouver to
escape the fantastic local prices. I'd made one trip "outside," a 10-day
journey there and back escorting a mental patient to Essondale near
New Westminster, and had managed a five-day patrol in the "police
boat," visiting several trappers' camps on Tagish Lake and the White
Pass' resort at Ben-My-Chree. The little boat was now beached on the
snowy shore of Atlin Lake and its motor stored away for the winter.
Atlin Lake should have been frozen over as it had been around -10°F
for almost two weeks, but strong winds blowing northward prevented
ice from forming. Atlin is some five to 12 miles wide, and about 90
miles long, the north end being in the Yukon. The water is glacial, and
even in mid-summer so cold that swimming is virtually impossible.
Survival time in winter would be measured in minutes.

During the first week in December I was approached by several
local people expressing concern about Vic Stevens, the resident White
Pass & Yukon Railway agent and caretaker at Taku Landing on Tagish

Lake. In the "open" season all supplies for Atlin came from the railway at Carcross via the paddlewheel steamer *Tutshi* some 85 miles along Tagish Lake to Taku Landing, thence over the shortest railway in the world across a narrow strip of land to Atlin Lake, then a five-mile crossing to Atlin by boat and barge.

Stevens, a philosophic gentlemanly type of 50 some years, lived alone at Taku Landing throughout the year, running the little railway during the operating season and caretaking its equipment during the winter. He had not been seen for several weeks. As it was usual for him to boat across to Atlin fairly frequently to visit friends and occasionally the government liquor store, it was conjectured that something might be amiss. Listening to the wind and looking at the whitecaps thrashing about the lake, I pointed out to those worrying about Vic that he could be waiting for a calm day. My logic was effective for a while. Unfortunately, gossip is persistent in a small town. It soon became clear that I was expected to do something as Vic might be ill, lying injured or dying as a result of some accident.

Apart from the pressure to take action, I probably fancied the role of rescuer. As a result on December 10 I decided to tackle the lake despite the high winds and rough, freezing-cold water. Father Dekeyzer, the local missionary priest, asked if he could accompany me. It was an offer I gladly accepted since he was a rugged individual and I needed moral support as well as weight in the bow. He had come from France a few years before, and often travelled with his Indian parishioners in small craft like mine.

The daylight hours are very brief in the north during December, so we started out early under leaden skies and with a wind that showed no signs of abating. Although the weather was unfavorable it didn't seem too bad when we were in the dock area, no doubt due to the protection of an island about a half mile offshore. I wore a police-issue bulky canvas-covered sheepskin coat and gave Father my canvas parka to cover his winter clothing. The old motor started easily and ran smoothly as we left the lea of the island, but I began to have doubts when we encountered the full force of the wind. The waves looked at least five or six feet high, breaking with nasty whitecaps all around us and spray scudding from their tops. However, we were able to angle across the turbulent water, and at full speed keep just ahead of the waves, although it seemed they would curl over our stern at any moment. Scotia Bay was the Atlin Lake end of the little railway Vic supervised, and we made record time getting there with nothing worse than frozen spray on our clothing.

Securing the boat, we walked through the snow along the railway toward Taku Landing and met Vic about halfway to his cabin, looking very fit. He said he had heard a motor and, curious too see what kind of fools would be on the lake in such weather, had set out to meet whomever they might be. He had more sense than to risk crossing to the town. He also had plenty of food, and had decided he could wait for freeze-up before visiting the community. He gave us a brew and a quick snack, then accompanied us back to Scotia Bay to wish us luck.

Gassing up, we headed out of the shelter of the Bay, aware that we had no daylight to spare. We were soon facing the howling wind and the waves that pranced to meet us in sets of three, each capped with white and looking about 10 feet high. I knew enough to quarter into them, but little else about this type of boating. Father Dekeyzer crouched in the bow, exposed to the full effect of the boat crashing into the waves. As we hit each one spray cascaded over him and back on me, freezing as it fell. Under more normal circumstances I would have bailed out unwanted water with a tobacco can, but it was impossible with the ice that formed so quickly. I was hoping Father was praying and took some comfort thinking that his calling gave him some advantage in that respect.

As we approached the middle of the lake conditions worsened. It seemed as though the wooden hull of the old boat could not stand much more of the pounding. Father Dekeyzer began to shout to me, but with the wind and his accent, I found it difficult to understand. Finally, I got the message: "Slow down, slow down, for God's sake!" interjecting his advice with a few words of French he probably did not learn in a seminary.

I had been running the motor full blast, not knowing any better. In addition, I was plagued with a lurking suspicion it might quit if not at full throttle. At reduced speed the crashing and pounding did subside to some extent. To my relief the aged Johnson kept sputtering right along, although spray continued to splash over us. I was very conscious of the light fading and that the boat had a heavy build-up of ice in its bottom. About then the good Father's prayers (or maybe mine) took effect, for there was a slight lull in the wind force. I gave the motor a bit more gas and we slipped in behind the island to comparative safety.

Taking stock as we reached shore, we found the boat very low in the water. No wonder. It was encrusted with ice and had several inches of it inboard. Our clothes and whiskers were thick with ice and the leather mitt of my steering hand had frozen firmly to the tiller. Quickly dragging the boat on to the beach, and grabbing the motor, Father and I dashed for the Detachment quarters. Here, over some very hot rums, we admitted to Bea and ourselves what a couple of idiots we were.

A day or two later the lake calmed down and ice began to form. When it had strengthened sufficiently Vic walked over it to visit his friends. I had learned a valuable lesson about "fools rushing in." Father Dekeyzer and I remained on excellent terms throughout the balance of his stay in Atlin, but for some reason he never asked to go out in my boat again.

In every policeman's career some experiences remain more vivid than others. They range from the humorous to upsetting, from the mysterious to tragic. Here is a selection of

MEMORIES THAT LINGER

ONLY ONE POLICEMAN? WELL, THERE WAS ONLY ONE RIOT!
by Deputy Commissioner Cecil Clark

In my 35 years on the B.C. Police Force I met many outstanding men from Commissioners to Constables. One was Dennis Cox who joined the force in the 1890s. Straight-backed from his military service and with a thick brogue from his Scottish-Irish background, he was all man.

Nanaimo in 1858, the year to which the B.C. Provincial Police traces its heritage. Always few in number, the policemen served from sailing ship days to the jet age.

Officers' duties ranged from chasing cattle rustlers to officiating at funerals. (See page 145.) Here policemen in the 1930s bring in the body of a Cariboo miner killed at Williams Creek.

A roadhouse at Lac La Hache in the early 1920s when Bill Riley was a Cariboo policeman. Like the ranch house he describes on page 148, plumbing was basic, with a chamber pot under the bed for emergencies.

He once told me that around 1910 when the new Malahat Drive between Victoria and Duncan was being built, John Haggerty's road gang used to celebrate pay night by getting drunk on rum. With rum at $2 a gallon from the Goldstream Hotel their state of euphoria usually ended in a free-for-all, using pick handles. Dennis would go out to Goldstream with a team and wagon and pick up the wounded and the principal aggressors. Of course, he noted, only one man was needed for a call of this nature. After all, there was only one riot!

It was on one of his birthdays that the boys in the Headquarters Office stood him a dinner at the Balmoral Hotel. At midnight the revellers phoned for a hack and, loading Dennis aboard, three of them — Constables Bob Armstrong, George Hood and Bob Owens — took the horse out of the shafts. Then through Victoria's principal street they pulled Dennis in triumph six blocks to his home on Pandora Avenue. Here, as Bob Owens related years later, Mrs. Cox "gave them hell for bringing her husband home in that condition."

Gad! If Inspector T. G. Wynn had heard, they'd all have been fired! Instead, Armstrong later headed the San Francisco Board of Fire Underwriters, George Hood became B.C.'s first Superintendent of Motor Vehicles, and Bob Owens retired as Inspector.

THE TELEPHONE GIRLS
by 1st Class Constable B. E. "Bal" Munkley

Before the advent of the automatic telephone and before the time when the B.C. Provincial Police had radio-equipped cars, and even earlier when in many cases members of the Force had no cars, local telephone operators gave invaluable assistance to police and the public.

In many cases, a switch in the telephone company's office controlled one or more red lights placed on top of high buildings to be clearly visible at night to a police officer patrolling streets and alleys. Even at Detachments manned by more than one policeman it was usual for only a single officer to be on night shift, especially if the population of the area was not large. He would spend most of his time "walking the beat."

Before leaving the office he would advise the telephone operator of where he was going. Then when she received a call requiring his attention she would obtain the gist of the message or complaint, and switch on the red light(s). As soon as the signal was spotted by the patrolling policeman he used the nearest phone to learn the details. Often such calls concerned matters near the officer and persons requiring his presence were frequently surprised by his prompt response.

At the smaller rural Detachments, where often only one man was posted, and where the geography of the district precluded use of the red light system, it was essential that the policeman work closely with the telephone operator. He would let her know when he left the police office and advise her of his return. This system enabled her to report complaints received during the time the police office was vacant. Of course an officer on a one-man Detachment had to sleep, but he could depend on the local night operator awakening him if he was needed.

I was stationed at Ladysmith on Vancouver Island for many years where policing was done by a two-man Detachment during most of my time. It was not unusual for us on a busy night to be directed to problems by the telephone operator who actually "stockpiled" the calls, and even established priority of their importance. Even if it was not a busy night we would not think of going anywhere without reporting our intended whereabouts to the telephone girls. On small Detachments policemen were on call around the clock, so any social life they enjoyed had to be dove-tailed with duties. If we went visiting, attended the local theatre (if there was one), or stepped into a cafe for a coffee, we religiously reported where we would be to the telephone office.

Believe me, without those "hello girls" we would have been hard pressed to perform police duties. Although it is not likely that any of the women who assisted us so greatly will ever read this item, I salute them all.

A MEMORABLE TROUBLEMAKER — AND THE SAD CONSEQUENCE
by Sergeant W. A. "Bill" Walker

I am sure that many of us in the B.C. Provincial Police had to contend with some character who caused trouble repeatedly. One such person I had to deal with while stationed at McBride was George Hughes. He came from the United States, had a lovely wife and two children and was employed by the Grand Trunk Pacific Railway. One would think from the background I have sketched that he might have been a better type than this story explains. Unfortunately, he had weaknesses concerning money and women, and would go to any length to indulge them. My first contact with him was in July 1914 when he came to my office and complained that he had lost $1,200 in a card game to the conductor and brakeman of a freight train. As he inferred he had been cheated, I told him there was nothing I could do unless he could prove his allegation, which he couldn't.

The money he had frittered away did not belong to him but to a woman in Calgary for whom he had been entrusted to sell some Home Oil shares which were then very active on the market due to the discovery of the Turner Valley oil fields south of Calgary. That night he had a fist fight with one of the men he had complained about, which I ignored as I felt the situation he had got himself into was because of his own folly. As he was in trouble regarding his misuse of the funds he was expected to turn over to the woman in Calgary, he prevailed upon the widow of a locomotive engineer who had three children to support to loan him $1,200 so he might meet his obligation. To my knowledge, he never repaid her.

My next brush with him was shortly after the outbreak of World War One. I received a telegram from Senior Constable H. McGuffy of Fort George (today's Prince George) asking that I arrest Hughes on a charge of wounding. He was the conductor of a freight train due to arrive at McBride at 6 o'clock in the morning and I took him into

Fort George, above, and McBride about 1912, typical railway communities born when the Grand Trunk Pacific was extended across Central B.C. in the early 1900s. McBride survived but Fort George became part of Prince George.

custody. I did not know what the circumstances of the wounding were as they had not been explained by the telegram. These I learned a few hours later from Al Robin, the McBride station agent.

He informed me that a man while attempting to board a freight about 10 miles east of McBride had fallen under the wheels and had both feet severed. As a caboose was being dispatched to the scene of the accident carrying the local physician, Doctor Taylor, I accompanied him. On our arrival we found a young man about 22, both of his feet hanging only by shreds of skin. The train involved in the grisly mishap had departed after its engineer had done what he could to arrest bleeding by tying cord about both ankles. The doctor gave the poor fellow a shot to ease his pain, and we got him into the caboose and headed for the small hospital at McBride. The injured man's name was Donnally. He was an amateur boxer and said that he did not wish to live without feet. Sadly, he did not have to face that prospect. He died about 5:00 the following morning.

What had led to the accident was that Donnally and two other young men had been with 20 other men in a boxcar of a freight bound for Edmonton. When the train was about 10 miles east of Fort George it had stopped so that an extra locomotive could be added to doublehead a grade. Hughes, who was the conductor, and a brakeman had entered the car and demanded a dollar a head from the transients for the privilege of riding the train. One man would not pay, so Hughes and the brakeman forced him out of the car. As the train got under way he tried to climb back on board. Hughes drew a revolver and shot him in the right leg below the knee. When the train neared McBride, Hughes, suspecting I might be waiting for him, had told the riders to jump off the side opposite to where I had posted myself and walk up the track. He promised that he would arrange to pick them up later.

It was a ruse on his part to prevent the witnesses to the shooting being interviewed. The train crews changed at McBride and the new personnel of the freight knew nothing of Hughes' worthless promise and, of course, had no intention of picking up the riders. When their train overtook Donnally and his two companions, it slowed for some reason. The three men, thinking it was pre-arranged by Hughes, had proceeded to clamber into open boxcars. Donnally slipped and fell under one of them.

At Hughes' preliminary hearing, Donnally's chums and the man who had been shot in the leg gave evidence. The case was committed for trial. Unfortunately, when it came before County Court Judge H. Robertson with Hughes electing speedy trial, Donnally's friends could not be located as witnesses. As there was no evidence offered except that of the man who had been shot, the judge had no alternative but to acquit Hughes.

AN UNFORGETTABLE FUNERAL
by Special Constable R. W. Smith

A policeman's duties are not always related to apprehending criminals. This statement was especially true of our service with the B.C. Provincial Police for we had many odd-ball assignments. Some of them were distasteful, but had to be taken care of.

In the 1940s I was a Special Constable on the Provincial Game Department motor launch which was also used for BCPP work. One day, skipper Corporal Roy E. Allan received a radio message from our Powell River office stating that an old woman had died at the Mission Hospital at Pender Harbour. She had been the wife of a former shipwright whose yard was located at Egmont at the mouth of Skookumchuck Rapids. Before dying she had requested that she be buried on a rise of ground behind the shipyard. We were instructed to carry out her wish.

On arriving at the hospital we signed for the body and placed it on the top deck of the launch. No coffin had been provided and the corpse was wrapped in canvas. Its blood had been substituted with formaldehyde and the pungent, sickening odor of the chemical bothered my activities in the galley, for as well as being a general hand I was also cook. One of the dishes I prepared was a favorite with Roy Allan, being Boston-style chowder made from fresh butter clams we gathered during our cruises. I was cooking up a batch of the chowder on our way to the Pender Harbour boatworks where we intended to have a coffin made. But before we reached that destination we received a distress call from a fishboat. By the time we were into Jervis Inlet in response the smell of the formaldehyde was mingling with that of my cooking and I wasn't feeling too good. Roy was in the pilothouse calling for more clam chowder — what a captain and what a stomach! Meanwhile, I was leaning over the stern rail heaving!

When we got to Pender Harbour it was late in the day, but Roy was able to arrange for a coffin to be made at the local boatworks. The shipwright must have worked most of the night for he had the casket ready by morning, even painted. We transferred the body to the box and set out for Egmont where the burial was to take place. On arrival we went about finding grave diggers and a minister. We were successful as to the diggers, but there was no preacher available and we had to settle for a Bible student. Our next step was to find a few people to attend the funeral, and pick wild flowers for the ceremony.

It was a cool overcast morning when our procession to the grave began, but the sun broke through the clouds and God created a beautiful day for our solemn task. The Devil, however, had his hand in. As the heat of the sun increased, the fresh paint on the coffin which was still tacky began to soften.

Leading the cortege was the Bible student, then came the pallbearers, bedaubed with paint. Following them was Corporal Allan in full uniform, marching ahead of 10 women carrying flowers. It was a simple funeral, but likely performed with more sincerity than many city counterparts. One of the local fishermen attending had made a wooden cross. All in all, the deceased got a fine send-off thanks to Roy.

You might think that this would be the end of our duties, but it was not. After the funeral we set out for Maude Bay, our home port, both of us needing a rest. Roy went to his home in Powell River while I did some routine ship chores. Two days later Roy returned with new orders. Among them were instructions from the Administrator's office that we pick up the personal effects of the woman we had buried.

This, we thought, was one of the easier jobs we had been given to do. We got under way for the old shipyard at Egmont and on arriving launched our dinghy and made for the beach. When we opened the back door of the old house where the woman had lived alone after the death of her husband, we were met by the smell of rotten fish so strong it was overpowering. Hanging on strings were literally hundreds of sardine can keys with the tin rolls of lids wound around them. Although there was evidence of a garden, it was apparent that the woman's diet had been sardines. What she had not eaten added to the offensive odor of the tin-wrapped keys.

As we gazed about in amazement in the gloomy kitchen, Roy and I began to scratch. We were being eaten alive by something. I placed a sheet of old newspaper on the floor and then took it outside to the brighter light. Fleas by the thousands! "Frank," Roy yelled, "get the hell out of here."

We raced in our torment for the beach, stripped off all our clothes, and waded into the ice-cold water. As we ducked into it the parasites ran up our bodies into our hair. We had to completely and repeatedly submerge ourselves to get rid of them. Luckily there was no one around or no doubt there would have been complaints about two nude policemen.

Roy was most concerned that the fleas would be carried aboard ship if we took our clothes with us, so we piled them in the dinghy. Having made sure we had rid our bodies of the pests, we clambered aboard stark naked to find other garments. We towed our infested uniforms in the dingy when we pulled away. As we left I have a vivid memory of Roy announcing: "Forget the woman's effects. We don't go there again until they fumigate the place."

I silently agreed.

JUST ONE OF THE GIRLS
by Corporal A. J. "Bert" Dillabough
When I was a rookie I was sent to Nanaimo on relief duty, and there I met Hugh Daubney. He left me alone in the office one beautiful sunny day, and the door being open as a result of the weather, I could see a very attractive girl approaching. Being young and single at the time I was very aware of the girl and thought how much I would like to know her.

To my surprise, she entered the office. "Hello," she said, "I'm Susie and I'm going to Vancouver for three days."

Why she should be telling me her intentions I couldn't imagine, so I naively asked her the reason.

"Silly!" she replied. "I work the 'line' and I'm here to check out."

She must have seen how perplexed I was, for she added: "You're new here, aren't you?"

I admitted I was. "Well, then," she laughed, "I'd better tell you in plain English! I'm a prostitute, and all the girls have to check with the police when they leave or return to Nanaimo. Get it?"

With that she came behind the counter where I stood gawking in embarrassment — and maybe blushing a bit — rummaged around and found a book. In it she wrote her name, the date, etc., and told me where to sign her entry. Boy, she must have thought I was dumb!

When Hugh returned and asked me if there had been anything doing. I acted the big shot and casually commented: "Nope. Just one of the girls who checked out!"

MY LONGEST RIDE
by Constable W. "Bill" Riley
While serving with the B.C. Provincial Police in the Cariboo, I prosecuted nine trappers for taking pelts before the season opened on January 1, 1922, and obtained convictions in all cases. One of the men was named Bill Whitely.

Later, when making a patrol on horseback on the North Bonaparte River trail, Bill Whitely, senior, stepped into my path. He was armed with a rifle and called me a s.o.b. and every other term of abuse he could lay his tongue to for having caused his son's conviction. He was very angry, and I was very scared.

I wished him "good day" and rode on up a steep hill. I didn't alter my pace to the top of the grade, and for the 200 feet I travelled before I was out of his sight I fully expected a bullet in my back every second. I can truthfully say I drew a deep breath of relief when I found myself out of his range. A game warden I knew, Albert Farey, had recently been shot in the back and killed in the Lillooet district under similar circumstances.

All in the life of a policeman.

But not all experiences were so unpleasant. One summer while on patrol I had to ask for overnight accommodation at a small ranch. After we had enjoyed a fine dinner, my hosts broke the news that I would have to sleep with their small son as they didn't have a spare bed. The privy was out of doors so a lard pail or some such container was left under the bed for emergencies. Some called it the "Goesunder."

The little fellow and I got undressed and ready for bed. He knelt down on the floor, resting his elbows on the bed. I thought he was saying his prayers and decided to follow his example or the kid might think badly of me. Down I got, put my hands together and tried to remember the Lord's prayer.

Suddenly the lad called out, "Hey, mister. What are you doing?"

"Same as you, son," I said.

"Gee, mister," he replied, "mom will give you heck in the morning. There's no pot on your side."

THE HORRORS OF PLANE CRASHES
by 1st Class Constable T. O. "Ted" Brue

Shortly after noon in the early summer of 1942 during World War Two an excited woman phoned the B.C. Provincial Police Detachment at Brighouse in Richmond to report that an airplane had crashed in her field about three miles south of the police office. I responded to the call with Sergeant Tom Herdman who was in charge of the Detachment.

The site was not difficult to find as it was marked with a column of smoke. On our arrival we found the plane, a Royal Canadian Air Force trainer, was almost consumed by fire. The intense heat prevented any action except obtaining statements from witnesses who indicated the craft had plunged straight down as though in a power dive.

What remained was gruesome. Three bodies could be seen, all charred extensively. The sweet, sickening odor of roasted human flesh filled the air. The force of the impact had buried the two motors so deep into the soft earth that they were never seen.

When the fire subsided and the wreckage was cool enough to approach we found the hearts of the victims had popped right through their chests. Sergeant Herdman instructed me to take each item as he handed it to me and make three separate piles of the effects of the airmen, and also three separate piles for their bodily remains. I wondered why, but soon learned the reason. When he took hold of one of the men's arms it came off his body as though it had never been attached. He handed the fire-charred arm to me. I confess I hesitated for a few seconds before I was able to take it. After that it became somewhat easier to handle the other remains.

By the time we had completed our duties I was off shift. Arriving home tired and hungry, I found we were having roast beef for our evening meal. I had a strong stomach, but my vivid remembrance of what I had experienced caused me to inform my wife that I could not eat that night.

The leather gloves I had been wearing at the crash site gave off the distinctive odor that sickened me. I tried to wash it out but gave up a few days later and threw them away.

PHANTOM OF THE GRAVEYARD
by 1st Class Constable George Phillips

One day a highly respected old-timer died in a rather remote area and was brought to Williams Lake for burial. Some weeks after the funeral a rumor developed that his death was not by natural causes but that he had been murdered by being poisoned. As the rumor persisted, we checked and found that no death certificate had been provided indicating the cause of demise, so we reported the circumstances to Victoria. In due course we were instructed to exhume the body. But it was to be done secretly so that the next of kin and the general public be unaware of the procedure. In consequence, one night a party consisting of the police under Sergeant McLinton, a coroner, a doctor with a flashlight in one pocket and a scalpel in the other, and a grave digger who happened to be a hunchback, went to the grave after dark and began to dig up the coffin.

Shortly after the digging commenced, a young man and his girl arrived in a car at the cemetery gate, switched off the lights, and proceeded to get cozy. The exhuming party crouched behind the tombstones waiting for the lovers to leave. After considerable wait it was evident that they had no intention of departing. The Sergeant became impatient and instructed the grave digger to go to the car and tell its occupants they were trespassing and would have to remove themselves. However, he didn't have the chance to speak to them.

They saw his hunchbacked figure silhouetted against the moon as he arose from behind a grave monument and untangled themselves in a hurry. Then they disappeared in a cloud of dust, no doubt convinced they had seen a genuine ghost. Without further interruption the digging was resumed. The coffin was brought up, opened, and the doctor performed an autopsy by his flashlight. He discovered that the cause of death was a perforated ulcer. The body was then lowered back into the grave.

LABOR PAINS? IN A MAN?
by 1st Class Constable J. A. "Jim" Williamson

Have you ever heard of a man having labor pains? Constable Harry Twist had them, or what seemed to be them, at the time his wife was expecting their first child. We were in Victoria in 1939 with the

Part of the Force's mounted troop at the opening of the B.C.
Legislative Assembly on February 17, 1932.

Mounted Troop during the Royal Visit and were billeted at Willows
Exhibition Park. There were about 12 of us, all sleeping in the same
room. For three nights Harry kept us awake pacing the floor complain-
ing of pains.

All those three nights we yelled at him, urging that he go to bed
so we could get some sleep. We ended up by throwing our boots, or
anything else we could reach, at him in our efforts to persuade him to
turn in. In the mornings we had the chore of sorting out our footwear
and other equipment from the conglomeration of what we had hurled.

Sergeant Ed Williamson, who was in charge, no doubt with
tongue-in-cheek convinced Harry that he was suffering from labor
pains in sympathy with his wife. Then Commissioner T. W. S. Parsons
heard about Harry's trouble and instructed that he be given leave and
a travel voucher so he could go to Vancouver to see his wife. But by
the time he reached Vancouver a baby daughter had been born. With
her arrival Harry's "labor pains" completely disappeared.

A VERY DUSTY MEMORY
by Corporal P. H. "Spike" Brown
While I was stationed at Victoria in 1935, Sergeant R. Harvey dispatched me to the Sooke area to search the residence of a very old
man who had died in hospital in Victoria. I was to locate, if possible,

his will and other papers and valuables to be taken into safe keeping. As far as we knew, the deceased was a bachelor and a recluse. The key to the premises was with a neighbor of the dead man. When I contacted him he suggested that he go with me. "You won't be prepared for what you will see," he said, "but I'm familiar with the situation and I think I can be of help."

Picking up a battery-powdered lantern, he accompanied me. When we approached the house it was in the gathering gloom of twilight, but I was able to see it was a one-floor structure located on what had been a small farm. There were agricultural implements standing around a sagging barn, all clearly unused for many years as trees were growing through their rusted mechanisms.

The neighbor unlocked the door and handed me the lantern. "You go directly into the kitchen," he explained, "that's where I found him before we took him to hospital. There are three rooms in the house. Take care."

There was a fetid odour about the place — one of mustiness and decay. We entered the kitchen which seemed reasonably clean. "He spent a lot of time in this room," said my companion as I began to search about. I opened a cupboard and a swarm of squealing mice scattered from the mouldering remains of sacks and packages of flour and other foodstuffs. I found nothing I sought in the kitchen. Taking the light from me, my guide shone it into the next room. "I don't think you'll ever have seen anything like this," he remarked.

He was right. Everything in what was a living room was grey — unbelievably grey — as though all it contained had been blanketed at least a quarter of an inch deep with some substance I first could not define. Then I realized it was dust! From the windows hung what I thought to be heavy black lace curtains, but proved to be cobwebs. From the kitchen through the room was a narrow path no wider than 18 inches from which the pall of dust had been swept. This path led to a bedroom. Half way along the path was a small island of cleanliness in which stood an armchair at the end of a large table. It was as thoroughly shrouded with dust as was the rest of the room, except for a small part of it immediately adjacent to the chair that had been kept free of the grey deposit, as had the chair. In its confines were an oil lamp, a pipe, tobacco pouch, matches, and a shallow tin into which the pipe's dottle had been tapped. "He read here," commented the man with me.

We followed the path to the bedroom and there found the same conditions as in the living room — massive cobwebs draped at the window, the same thickness of dust in all parts except for an island in which was a bed. I had to search the house, and wherever I walked, apart from the kitchen, I left footprints when I left the path. When I opened a desk dust fell from it as though it had been accumulating for decades, which was confirmed by the man working with me. Every book, box, easel-framed picture, or whatever I moved had to have the clinging dust shaken from it before I could recognize what it might be. I have often regretted that I did not have a flash camera with me that night to record the scene, for those I have told about it have had difficulty believing me.

What I discovered from my investigation was the former resident had been an officer in the Royal Navy, and that he was titled. There was no will, and only a few documents of importance. I gathered what I thought would be of relevance, together with what valuables I could find, such as a gold watch, money and so forth. The neighbor offered coffee at his home and while we drank he recounted what he knew of the man who had lived in the dust-ridden house.

"He was there when I bought my place about 30 years ago," he related. "As far as I know he had been there at least 20 years before. Never once did I see him leave his property. He had an arrangement with me to pick up what he needed from the stores, and to get his mail. I can't remember him ever receiving anything but advertising flyers and envelopes bearing some sort of a crest and English stamps, posted from London, and they came regularly every four months. After he got one he would give me a postal money order to cash for him, always the same amount — $150.

He paid me to keep him supplied with firewood. My wife and I often asked him to visit and have a meal with us, but he never would, so we gave up. Sometimes she'd take him a cake or a pie and such things, but he'd meet her at his door and wouldn't allow her in. He'd never talk about himself. I only got into the house a few times when something went wrong that he needed my help to fix."

What prompted that erstwhile naval officer to live as he had for 50 or more years from the time he must have been in his 30s, was one of the mysteries I have puzzled over ever since. What does your imagination suggest?

UPSETTING EXPERIENCES
by 1st Class Constable B. W. "Barry" Jones

During the four years from 1938-42 I was in charge of the one-man Maillardville Detachment which embraced Coquitlam Municipality. There were among my varied experiences some which, to say the least, were not conducive to restful slumber. Although of grisly nature, they were representative of duties which many of us in the Force were required to do. They are therefore offered as a reflection of one phase of our work.

The sudden death of a local youth after a Saturday night party resulted in my first attendance at a post mortem in a New Westminster hospital. It was necessary, owing to his age and no previous medical history suggesting a reason for death. The pathologist performing the physical investigation was most efficient, and in no time had the subject's chest cavity and other areas open. As will be appreciated, since this was my initial post mortem, I was more than a little squeamish, especially when the pathologist removed the heart and proceeded to show it to me. Holding it in his gloved hand, he explained that death had resulted from the organ's condition. I was horrified when he accidently dropped it and it fell into the hand of the body lying face up on the slab. Then I was further distressed when it slid from that position to the floor. From there the examiner retrieved it without, I swear, missing a single word of his lecture to me. It was a long time before I could erase the memory of that first post mortem or forget the odor of formaldehyde which seemed to linger in my nostrils.

The most bizarre of my experiences concerned an aged widow who lived alone in her small, well-kept home on Brunette Street. I was called to investigate her possible need of assistance. A light had been noticed in her house for several nights in exactly the same location, but she had not been seen for days. I was unable to obtain response to my knockings on front and rear doors, and entered the premises with some difficulty through an unlatched window.

Almost at once I was aware of the sickly-sweet odor with which I am sure most police officers have become familiar at some time in their service. It is especially noticeable in warm, enclosed areas — and we were in the middle of a fairly hot summer.

My fears were proven. On entering a bedroom I found a lamp burning on a table. In the bed was the body of the woman lying on her back. On viewing the face I recoiled appalled. Nearly all of it was missing.

At that moment I was startled by something brushing past my legs. From under the bed had come two cats — first a large one, then a smaller one. I followed them to the kitchen and threw the door open. They fled into the rear yard and disappeared.

That was the last I saw of them. They had, of course, starved to the point where they had dined on the only available food.

Verdict of the inquest was death by natural causes. But since that time I have, understandably, never been fond of cats.

SATURDAY NIGHT IN THE OLD FISHING TOWN
by 2nd Class Constable Glenn A. Bassett

In 1948 I had just completed my training in the Force's academy at Victoria and was posted to Richmond, complete with new uniform of which I was very proud. The commercial fishing community of Steveston was part of Richmond and we had to take turns at "foot patrol" from 8:00 p.m. to 4:00 a.m. on Saturday nights. They were often lively because the fishermen and cannery workers who were hard workers were also inclined to raise a bit of hell after having a few or more drinks.

Moncton Street was the main drag of Steveston. One Saturday night I was making my shift on foot patrol, resplendent in my new uniform with its brass and leather polished to a degree that would meet any inspection. The street was as quiet as a graveyard. But this condition was to change, for between two buildings I observed a man who was a local repeater in our cells. He was obviously in an advanced state of intoxication and still had with him a half-consumed bottle of Scotch. He was mean and tough when he was drunk, and although I did my best to persuade him to get off the street, he persisted in giving me a bad time.

I knew the hotel's beer parlor would be closing soon and I wanted him out of the way by then. However, he refused to go home and struck me a hard blow on my chest. I responded by giving him a push which overbalanced him and he fell on his back. I then took advantage of his position to endeavour handcuffing his wrists for there seemed no other way to subdue him. In the process he struck me a sharp blow to a most sensitive part of my anatomy. I retaliated with my billy.

By now people who lived above stores and other business establishments had heard the sounds of my struggles with the inebriated and belligerent man and were looking out windows and yelling, "Fight, fight, fight!" The hotel's beer parlor was emptying and Moncton Street was filling with its patrons, all more or less in their cups. A ring of boisterous and unfriendly persons crowded around me and the man I was by now sitting on while trying to handcuff him. I was kicked in the back half a dozen times by friends and relatives of my fighting drunk. Then a young woman hit me on the head with a 12-pack of beer. I can still remember seeing stars!

Fortunately, an off-duty Vancouver City policeman who was visiting in Steveston alerted the Detachment of the trouble I was having. Then he identified himself to the crowd and announced that help was on the way. He stood by me sharing the verbal abuse I was getting, his actions making me feel proud that I belonged to a police fraternity.

The sound of a siren could now be heard, and the louder it got the more the crowd dispersed. Finally, the police car arrived. By then there were only five people on Moncton Street — Constables Dick Stone and Ken Brand, the Vancouver City policeman, my prisoner and me.

My lovely new uniform looked very sad — ripped, scraped and blood stained from head to toe, but only to be expected under the circumstances.

The next day I tracked down the woman who had hit me over the head with the case of beer. She was from Manitoba and visiting friends in Richmond. Her explanation was that she thought I was a soldier fighting with a civilian, and that she was always sympathetic toward civilians. Magistrate Palmer did not accept her explanation. He fined her $100 for assaulting a police officer. But she had the last word. She complained to me that three bottles of beer had been broken when she hit me on the head!

TWO NATURAL DEATHS — WITH DIFFERENT CONSEQUENCES
by Corporal P. H. "Spike" Brown

A man who was prominent in one town where I was stationed, and one of the breed who considered the police to be much lower than his position on the social ladder, died one night in the bed of a woman who was not his wife. His paramour had to notify us since she had no alternative. The local doctor, who was also the coroner, satisfied himself that death was by natural cause, a heart attack. So to avoid embarrassment to the man's wife who was a very fine woman with no suspicions of his infidelity, and to his children, we let it be known that he had died on the street between his place of business and his home. No one was the wiser.

The other case had an unexpected consequence — for me at least. It happened while I was stationed in Victoria and detailed by Sergeant Dick Harvey to investigate the death of a hunter who had died from a heart attack in a field near Sidney. In his bag were several quail and a brace of pheasants. Not knowing what to do with the birds as there was no convenient way to preserve them, I offered them to the farmer who had discovered the man's body.

He refused them, saying he had all the game he could use. He urged me to take them as he was positive relatives of the deceased would not wish them due to the circumstances. They made a tasty meal for my wife and me and two friends we invited to the repast.

Two days later the son of the hunter presented himself at the police office, saw Sergeant Harvey, and demanded the birds. The Sergeant asked for my explanation of where they might be, to which I said that as I thought they would spoil I had "disposed" of them. The Sergeant diplomatically handled the situation, but after the young man had left, took me to task to a degree that made me decidedly uncomfortable. However, it seemed his scolding was a matter of routine.

Not long after he gave me some unsolicited hints as to the best way to prepare game fowl for the oven. Then, evidently as puzzled as I had been, added: "Who would think a member of the family would ask for them?"

A "VINTAGE" REMEMBRANCE
by 1st Class Constable George Phillips

I was stationed with the B.C. Provincial Police at Lake Cowichan in the late 1940s. After an absence of some years I returned to that Vancouver Island village to spend a few days on vacation. While walking down one of its streets I was stopped by an old fellow who offered me his hand. As I shook it, I didn't recognize him until he smilingly asked, "Remember the time you pinched me for bootlegging?"

Then my time-dimmed memories, stirred by the clue he gave, prompted my reply, "I sure do, Ralph."

That "pinch" took place in either 1948 or 1949. Lake Cowichan was the supply center of a large logging-sawmill complex employing several hundred men, and the beer parlor in the Riverside Inn was then the only licensed liquor outlet in the area. As the closest government liquor store was at Duncan, about 25 miles away, it was only to be expected that a number of local people were encouraged to engage in bootlegging to meet the demands of the thirsty, hard-working loggers — and others. We were aware of such activities, but were less than enthusiastic about enforcing the rather archaic liquor laws.

There were occasions, however, when we had no choice but to

prosecute. One of the prosecutions involved an elderly man named Ralph who was a decent little chap. The modest profit he made from his illegal sales of liquor was used to augment his meagre war pension. He operated from his residence on the main street of the town.

One day we received a phone call from a woman who lived across the street from Ralph. She reported that she had been watching his house and strongly suspected he was bootlegging. As a result I called on him and told him we had received a complaint, and warned him that if there was another it would bring police action. He said he felt he was getting a fair break and for the next three or four months all was quiet. Then I had another call from the same woman who said she had been watching Ralph's place from her front window. She was now firmly convinced he was bootlegging. I promised to take the necessary steps.

The following Saturday night, Constable Stan Hodges and I raided Ralph's home and found several men in the living room enjoying a quiet drink. Among those present were four very good friends of mine who need only be identified as Jack, Bert, Bill, and a member of the Village Council. We told Ralph he would be arraigned in court on Monday morning and seized his stock of liquor.

The Police Detachment at that time consisted of two rooms in the Riverside Inn. One of them was used as an office and for court proceedings; the other was my bedroom. Into its clothes closet we placed the confiscated bottles, using it as an exhibit locker. Among the items seized was a bottle of rum with a measuring jigger in its neck, and a bottle of rare imported wine.

Ralph appeared in court on Monday, pleaded guilty, and was fined $300, the liquor to be impounded. When the court closed, Ralph turned to the magistrate and said, "You know, Colonel, when the boys raided me Saturday night they cleaned me right out and I haven't got a drop to drink. Would it be O.K. if I take that part bottle of rum with the jigger?"

Lake Cowichan affairs being always on an informal basis with less than "by the book" approaches in most cases, the magistrate replied that Ralph's request seemed reasonable. The convicted bootlegger placed the bottle under his coat and hurried happily home.

When he had gone the magistrate asked me how we usually disposed of seized liquor. I told him that on previous occasions my instructions had been to pour it down the toilet. Pondering this, he then wanted to know if my instructions specified how the liquor was to enter the toilet and if any special toilet was designated. On being informed that I knew of no restrictions bearing on his questions, he replied that if that was case he would select a bottle of fine Scotch from the impounded stock and make personally sure of its disposal in accordance with the generalities of my instructions. He placed the whisky in his pocket and left the office.

I made out my Form 19 report covering the amount of liquor taken into custody and thought that would be the end of the matter. I couldn't have been more wrong!

That same night after the beer parlor closed I made my usual patrol around town before retiring. When I returned to the Inn I was met by my four friends: Jack, Bert, Bill, and the Village Councilman. They had come to the conclusion that inasmuch as they had paid for a drink each at Ralph's place on Saturday night and didn't get the chance to imbibe, they were entitled to compensation from the stock seized from him. Their interpretation of the circumstances seemed to make sense, so we disposed of some of the hard liquor and also the bottle of rare imported wine.

I figured that this was definitely the end of the case, but again I was wrong. Not long afterward I received a phone call from Corporal Les Jeeves at Duncan Detachment. He advised that I was going to have a visit the following afternoon from the Commissioner of the Force, Roger Peachey, and Inspector Robert Owens, Officer Commanding A Division to which I was attached.

When I hung up the phone, I thought, "My God, suppose they want to check the liquor exhibits? It certainly was to be expected in the course of a Detachment inspection! There being no liquor store in town, I scurried around among my friends and managed to replenish the exhibits with the exception of the bottle of wine. I phoned Duncan Detachment and explained my plight to Constables Jack Meredith-Jones and Vic Fawdrey. With their usual esprit de corps they offered to obtain the wine at the local government vendor.

Soon they called back to say the Duncan store didn't carry that brand of wine, but there was an escort taking a prisoner to Nanaimo and a check of the liquor store in that city would be made. To my great relief they phoned later to say they had been able to obtain the wine, and I soon had it locked in the clothes closet with the other exhibits.

Peachey and Owens arrived the following day and during their inspection I was required to unlock the "exhibit locker." They were most favorably impressed with the great care we took in securing seized spirits.

At their request, I then took them around town to meet some of the residents, including the magistrate and the Village Councilman. Naturally, those two persons were high in their praise of the efficient policing within the community. When we returned to the Inn, and just before they were to leave for Victoria, I asked Commissioner Peachey and Owens if I could offer them a glass of fine wine. Bob Owens was never one to turn down a drink. They accepted my invitation.

A short time afterward I watched them driving down the dusty road out of the village. I thought that some day I'd tell them the story about the wine, but sad to say it was not to be. It was their last visit to Lake Cowichan. Not long after, the old Force was disbanded, and since then both those fine gentlemen have long gone to their last reward.

On looking back, we'd like to think we used some common sense and compassion in our law enforcement. While so doing, we met some wonderful people and made some life-long friends.

In Memorium

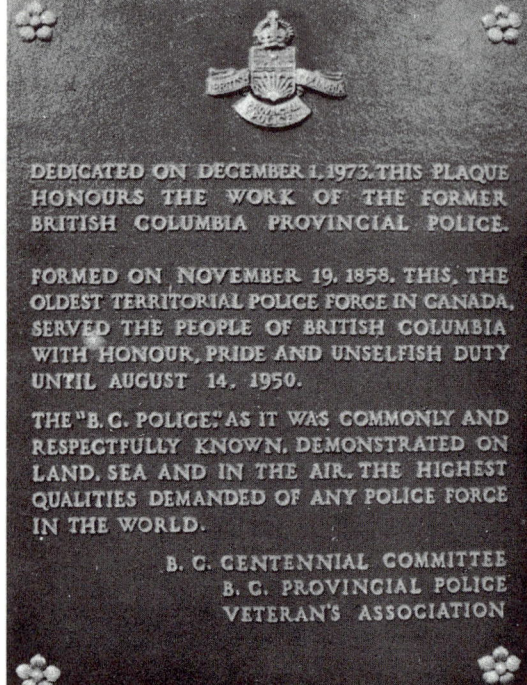

Despite the B.C. Provincial Police's almost century of service, there is virtually no official tribute to them or to the 13 who sacrificed their lives on duty. This plaque at the Provincial Museum-Archives in Victoria is inconspicuous on a wall in a sunken garden. The policemen deserve a more impressive memorial.

POLICEMEN WHO DIED ON DUTY

Constable John D.B. Ogilvie, Bella Coola, May 1865

Constable John Lawson, Wildhorse Creek, April 1867

Constable John T. Ussher, Kamloops, December 1879

Constable Geoffrey H. Aston, Okanagan Lake, March 1912

Constable Alexander Kindness, Clinton, May 1912

Constable Henry Westaway, Union Bay, March 1913

Constable George Stanfield, Grand Forks, June 1920

Constable Arthur W. Mable, Kamloops, September 1926

Constable Percival Carr, Merritt, May 1934

Inspector Wm. J. Service, Prince Rupert, July 1938

Sergeant Robert Gibson, Prince Rupert, July 1938

Constable Clifford A. Prescott, Princess Royal Island, June 1939

Constable Frank Clark, Victoria, November 1941

A selection of other *HERITAGE HOUSE* titles:

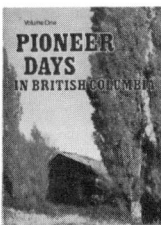

The PIONEER DAYS IN BRITISH COLUMBIA Series
Every article is true, many written or narrated by those who, 100 or more years ago, lived the experiences they relate. Each volume contains 160 pages in large format magazine size (8½ x 11"), four-color covers, some 60,000 words of text and over 200 historical photos, many published for the first time.
A continuing Canadian best seller in four volumes which have sold over 75,000 copies. Each volume, $10.95

WHITE SLAVES OF THE NOOTKA
On March 22, 1803, while anchored in Nootka Sound on the West Coast of Vancouver Island, the *Boston* was attacked by "friendly" Nootka Indians. Twenty-five of her 27 crew were massacred, their heads "arranged in a line" for survivor John Jewitt to identify. Jewitt and another survivor became 2 of 50 slaves owned by Chief Maquina, never knowing what would come first — rescue or death.
The account of their ordeal, published in 1815, remains remarkably popular. New Western Canadian edition, well illustrated. 128 pages. $9.95

THE DEATH OF ALBERT JOHNSON: Mad Trapper of Rat River
Albert Johnson in 1932 triggered the greatest manhunt in Canada's Arctic history. In blizzards and numbing cold he was involved in four shoot-outs, killing one policeman and gravely wounding two other men before being shot to death.
This revised, enlarged edition includes photos taken by "Wop" May, the legendary bush pilot whose flying skill saved two lives during the manhunt. Another Canadian best seller. $7.95

OUTLAWS AND LAWMEN OF WESTERN CANADA
These true police cases prove that our history was anything but dull. Chapters in 160-page Volume Three, for instance, include Saskatchewan's Midnight Massacre, The Yukon's Christmas Day Assassins, When Guns Blazed at Banff, and Boone Helm — The Murdering Cannibal.
Each of the three volumes in this Canadian best seller series is well illustrated with maps and photos and four-color photos on the covers. Volume One, $8.95; Volume Two, $8.95; Volume Three, $9.95

B.C. PROVINCIAL POLICE STORIES: Mystery and Murder
from the Files of Western Canada's First Lawmen
The B.C. Police, born in 1858, were the first lawmen in Western Canada. During their 90 years of service they established a reputation as one of the most progressive police forces in North America. All cases in this best selling title are reconstructed from archives and police files by ex-Deputy Commissioner Cecil Clark who served on the force for 35 years.
Volume One: 16 chapters, many photos, 128 pages. $8.95
Volume Two: 22 chapters, many photos, 144 pages. $9.95

B.C. BACKROADS
This best selling series contains complete information from Vancouver through the Fraser Canyon to Cache Creek, east to Kamloops country and north to the Cariboo. Also from Vancouver to Bridge River-Lillooet via Whistler. Each book contains mile-by-mile route mileage, history, fishing holes, wildlife, maps and photos.
Volume One — Garibaldi to Bridge River Country-Lillooet. $9.95
Volume Three — Junction Country: Boston Bar to Clinton. $9.95
Thompson-Cariboo: Highways, byways, backroads. $9.95

An Explorer's Guide: MARINE PARKS OF B.C.

To tens of thousands of boaters, B.C.'s Marine Parks are as welcome and convenient as their popular highway equivalents. This guide includes anchorages and onshore facilities, trails, picnic areas, campsites, history and other information. In addition, it is profusely illustrated with color and black and white photos, maps and charts.

Informative reading for boat owners from runabouts to cabin cruisers. 200 pages.   *$12.95*

GO FISHING WITH THESE BEST SELLING TITLES

HOW TO CATCH SALMON — BASIC FUNDAMENTALS

The most popular salmon book ever written. Information on trolling, rigging tackle, most productive lures, proper depths, salmon habits, how to play and net your fish, downriggers, where to find fish.

Sales over 120,000. 176 pages. $5.95

HOW TO CATCH SALMON — ADVANCED TECHNIQUES

The most comprehensive advanced salmon fishing book available. Over 200 pages crammed full of how-to tips and easy-to-follow diagrams. Covers all popular salmon fishing methods: mooching, trolling with bait, spoons and plugs, catching giant chinook, and much more.

A continuing best seller. 192 pages. $11.95

HOW TO CATCH CRABS: How popular is this book? This is the 11th printing, with sales over 90,000. $4.95

HOW TO CATCH BOTTOMFISH: Revised and expanded. $4.95

HOW TO CATCH SHELLFISH: Updated 4th printing. 144 pages. $3.95

HOW TO CATCH TROUT by Lee Straight, one of Canada's top outdoorsmen. 144 pages. $4.95

HOW TO COOK YOUR CATCH: Cooking seafood on the boat, in a camper or at the cabin. 8th printing. 192 pages. $4.95

FLY FISH THE TROUT LAKES

with Jack Shaw

Professional outdoor writers describe the author as a man "who can come away regularly with a string when everyone else has been skunked." In this book, he shares over 40 years of studying, raising and photographing all forms of lake insects and the behaviour of fish to them.

Written in an easy-to-follow style. 96 pages. $7.95

A CUTTHROAT COLLECTION: B.C. experts pool their knowledge and experience to unravel the mysteries and methods of catching this elusive fish. $5.95

SALMON FISHING BRITISH COLUMBIA: Volumes One and Two

Since B.C. has some 7,000 miles of coastline, a problem to its 400,000 salmon anglers is where to fish. These books offer a solution. Volume One includes over 100 popular fishing holes around Vancouver Island. Volume Two covers the Mainland Coast from Vancouver to Jervis Inlet. Both include maps, gear to use, best times, lures and a tackle box full of other information.

Volume One — Vancouver Island. $9.95
Volume Two — Mainland Coast: Vancouver to Jervis Inlet. $11.95
